J S Harry | Not Finding Wittgenstein

Peter Henry Lepus Poems

GIRAMONDO POETS

J S Harry | Not Finding Wittgenstein

First published 2007
for the Writing & Society Research Group
at the University of Western Sydney
by the Giramondo Publishing Company
PO Box 752
Artarmon NSW 1570 Australia
www.giramondopublishing.com

Designed by Harry Williamson
Typeset by Andrew Davies
in 10/17 pt Baskerville

Printed and bound by Southwood Press
Distributed in Australia by Tower Books

National Library of Australia
Cataloguing-in-Publication data:

Harry, J.S.
Not finding Wittgenstein.

ISBN 978 1 920882 20 4.

I. Title.

A821.3

For Sarah, Andrew, Sally, and Bill

Previous poetry collections:

the deer under the skin (1971)
Hold, for a little while, and turn gently (1979)
A Dandelion for Van Gogh (1985)
The Life on Water and the Life Beneath (1995)
J.S. Harry – Selected Poems (1995)
Sun Shadow, Moon Shadow (2000; 2nd ed. 2001)
If...And the Movable Ground, (2004)

Acknowledgements

Angus & Robertson and Paper Bark Press for the *Peter Henry Lepus* poems in *The Life on Water and the Life Beneath*, some of which were published in the same or different forms in *Meanjin*, *Phoenix Review*, *Salt* and *Southerly*. Penguin Books Australia (*J.S. Harry – Selected Poems*) for 'National Shrines (Nobody Wins at a Ritual?)'. Vagabond Press for the poems in *Sun Shadow, Moon Shadow*, Stray-Dog Editions No. 3 (2000 and 2001), and previously *HEAT*, *Meanjin*, *Southerly* and *Verse* (USA).

Poems in the third and fourth section have not been published in single-volume form. Thanks to the editors of the following journals or anthologies, in which some of these poems have appeared (sometimes in slightly different forms): *Australian Book Review*, *Best Australian Poetry 2005*, ed. Peter Porter, (UQP), *famous reporter*, *HEAT*, *postwest*, *Southerly*, *www.poetryinternational.org*, *Best Australian Poems 2006,* ed. Dorothy Porter, (Black Inc) and *five bells,* Special Poetry Festival Edition, Spring 2006.

And sometimes when people went on the roads
they changed their lives.
BOB HUDSON, ABC RADIO, 19 JUNE 1991

In principle, philosophy can always
go astray, which is the sole reason why it can go forward.
THEODORE ADORNO, *Negative Dialectics*

It is more important that a proposition be interesting
than that it be true.
A.N. WHITEHEAD, *Adventures of Ideas*

If one does not hope, one will not find the unhoped-for,
since there is no trail leading to it, and no path.
HERACLITUS

Contents

Introduction

Biographical Notes on Peter Henry Lepus

His mother, an extremely well-read and well-educated rabbit of Creole ancestry, named Peter Henry Lepus after a character in a book of old Creole folktales, *L'Histoire de Pierre Henri Lepus*. However he is a British rabbit and his mother has always called him *Peter* Lepus, rather than Pierre, although pronouncing the 'Lepus' with a slight French accent, out of deference to the Creole, so that the final syllable sounds the same as the vowel at the end of the French word 'chou' and has a pleasant sound when you call it across a grassy meadow in the evening. Sometimes she calls him Peter Henry, or Peter L. Most frequently she simply calls him Peter. He has become accustomed to pricking his ears to all of these names.

He has, at times, been something of a disappointment to his mother, possibly as he has turned out to have a somewhat different character from the Creole hero after whom he was named.

It is uncertain whether the Creole hero's family name was originally 'Lapsus' and the 'p' became somehow disconnected, losing itself in one of those gaps in time or memory, emerging unpredictably (much later) on the ground of the word's wornaway, first 's', or whether the name was always 'Lapus' – and the hero's mother found it ugly.

Either way, she was the one who changed the name to 'Lepus'. Her reading of confused books, the texts of which did not discriminate between the rabbits and the hares but conflated them into a single species, might have led her to a conclusion about the ways in which diacritical language was constructed by *homo sapiens*, the errors of which she commemorated ironically: the Creole rabbit family's 'Lapsus' – or 'Lapus' – becoming 'Lepus'.

Unlike his namesake, Peter Lepus grew up in the English countryside of the early twentieth century, where he was exposed, to a degree, to the culture of that time. He was put into a children's book at an early age and has travelled extensively.

Occasionally finding perplexing drawings of himself torn from the pages of the rare, first English-language edition of *Peter Henry Lepus* (where the surname is misspelt on spine and title page) on the walls of the Great Rabbit Burrows of France and Germany, Peter Lepus was also puzzled to find images of his grey-brown self nailed to the lower well-nibbled boles of trees in more distant countries. Sometimes these images of himself had small round holes in them. (Some biographers have speculated Peter Lepus's later interest in philosophy may have stemmed from the sight of such 'almost-perfect near-circular enclosures'. There is ground for disputing this.)

It was not to be predicted that when *The Tale of Peter Henry Lepus* had reached the ears of almost every rabbit household in Britain, it would be reinvented, so it could enter burrows in diverse new places, including, later, Spain, nor that its small rabbit persona should be analysed, for improprieties 'mental and moral'*, in an essay-*cum-laude* by Graham Greene, or psychoanalysed, even though somewhat disrespectfully, by some post-modern students of Freud.

Peter Henry Lepus, the book of the early childhood, became a classic and a standard text for Children's

Literature courses. However, as Peter L. never hopped, as a student, through those particular hedgerows, he remained largely ignorant of his 'life' in other people's psyches and of his 'status' in those remote, perspicaciously observed yet for him somehow 'bladeless' fields.

There is a tale passing as truth in Baton Rouge today, in rap song form, among the musos in some of the smokier bars, that Peter L. met Wittgenstein in Vienna in nineteen hundred and two and disputed with him on the aerodynamics for an airborne bicycle, with trainer wheels for learner flyers.

In some raps, the bike is a winged, prototype-jet (two-wheeler), with optional extra ailerons for would-be high-flyers.

This fine flying 'history', the details of which the singers vary endlessly, apparently unconsciously, steers away from biographers' facts and dates, at almost all its points. (Perhaps the tale and its tellers share, with the hare family, a rabbity habit of wiping one's chin in scorn on those combinations of things – or states of affairs – for which, for whatever reason, one has contempt? Including death?)

In nineteen hundred and two the young Wittgenstein was being educated at home. He was thirteen and had thought about suicide. He had not yet begun to study engineering. His knowledge of the mechanics of the wheel was slim. All he had managed to design, even according to rumour, was a slightly-working copy of a sewing machine. His interest in aerodynamics surfaced only in nineteen hundred and seven, after he had spent three (miserable) years at school and a further three (unhappy) terms at Tech. He did not attempt to acquire the maths for aeronautical design before nineteen hundred and eight.

Peter L. had, up to nineteen hundred and two, no awareness of aeronautics and little knowledge of mechanical engineering.

Early family portraits, dated nineteen hundred and two in brown ink on the back, show a young and tense Peter Lepus, scenting danger, peering stiffly out at the third year of the twentieth century, from behind the ampler bodies of the older aproned rabbits in his family, as if he feels he needs their bulk and kick-power to protect him.

He appears far too small, in the year of the brown-ink portraits, to have been able to travel to London, stow away on a ship, or reach Vienna by himself.

Around about the time A.N. Whitehead and Bertrand Russell were working their way towards *Principia Mathematica* (and perhaps before Wittgenstein had arrived in England, to 'discover', and become, briefly, a student of, Bertrand Russell), Peter Henry Lepus was provoked into trying to use his mind...

It is perhaps from this period onward that his sense of deracination and disorientation becomes more pronounced...

* This may be a reference to Peter Lepus's later, somewhat infelicitous studies in philosophy; the latter discipline, according to Rush Rhees, was known at Cambridge as 'Mental and Moral Sciences'.

First Poems

Lapin on the Loose

I 'Under Drought'

Like a pirated edition
of the book of himself
the eponymous Peter Henry Lepus
gets dumped in Australia.

Forty per cent of it
is 'under drought'. Peter Henry
has never been 'under drought' before –
only under fences & gates.
He wonders if it is anything like
being 'under the doctor', as a man he met
by the railroad track told Peter
the man's missus was. The Australia
Peter is in looks very large & brown.
Rock-piled hills wear hats of shade
where rabbits are lying around.
Somnolent rabbits with sick red eyes
stir sluggishly to glare at him – an interloper,
in exile. *We are replicas of the spirits*
of rabbits who have died
by mosquito-bite disease,
they inform.   He
has never heard of mosquitoes – or bite-disease –
& doesn't much care   why
strange rabbits died.

Lean, listless, cotton-coloured animals,
        with their fur hanging down
in draggly oily curls – as if their mothers
hadn't been near them with brushes for centuries –
bleat languidly at him, from a stony
cotton-coloured ground. Some – the more alert –
        are clustered
round a dry, white-crusted lake.
You can't drink here – it's salt,
they baa importantly at him. They
are waiting for a ship
to go to the Middle East,
but there has been a war on –
        their 'holiday'
has been put off; the sheep-
tour advisers bleat:
        it will be months
before their 'cruise''s number
comes up. Peter
        isn't thirsty. Baas
are a bore. *Where is my mother?* he yells,
from the middle of a sand dune's
slope, standing – to see if he can see her
from higher up. This ground is hot.
Then he squats.
        He is bitten, by small black
maddened, running things
        which stink, when squashed. Enraged,

more & more of them pour upward
out of a hole. *There are thousands of us*
underneath you, they sign
six-legged at him. *You are sitting*
on our house. He moves out. Fast.
Fast is what he has to do:
there are no grass blades,
cucumber frames, or radishes,
out here in the fields of sand,
on the Desert of Sense.
Nothing to eat, he moans
as he mouths the roasted sand.
It is so horrid they don't even need
        fences & gates   to try
to keep a good rabbit out.

2 A Good Rabbit?

He meets a travelling
flock of boastful galahs
who tell him they are poets of the feather.
We are the mistresses & masters
of beauty, they yell. *Come with us*
to the Balmain
Brolga's & we will show you
how to strip
shed leaves &
nest in holes,
but Peter doesn't believe
they know what they are screeching of...
What is beauty? Is it grass?
They do not ask him
to come to *grass* with them...*Where is grass?...*
    Weeds   would do.

One of the unwell rabbits drags itself past.
Are there any dandelions round here?
Peter asks it politely...
    A weed is not a weed
    to a rabbit: it is food...
or a place where the baby beans
hang down, crisp & low – rattling
the old beans' leaves – for a game in the sunset,
to annoy them –

so a rabbit on its hindlegs
can reach up & snap them off?

But the rabbit is too busy –
it is going down a long dark tunnel inside itself
to a ground
where it has never been before. The eyes
it looks at the world with are losing interest.
It does not answer Peter. Its whiskers quiver.
Peter leans closer to hear. *How beautiful*
grass is...it breathes, almost with no air.
Then it gives a long slow exhalation
as its lungs say goodbye to the world.
Peter has never seen a dead rabbit before.
He goes round it on all fours sniffing.
This rabbit looks just like the live ones.
Perhaps it will wake up, presently,
& talk to him.
But the rabbit does not wake up,
so, after a little wait, Peter Lepus moves off.

'South' Country – in 'Value-Judgement' Land –

I

Old Mrs Rabbit told him
always to keep
his bump of locality
about him. He was never too sure
what she meant: it seemed to shift around
depending on
where *she* was. Perhaps she kept it hidden
safe – for him –
& it only worked
when *she* sat down?
                    Anyrate, now, he seems
to have lost it.
                    At the top of a good
rabbit's back-scratching post, he comes
to a square bit of lettered wood
                                        which spells:
YOU ARE STANDING ON FORTY-THREE BLENDS
OF DUSTED-OFF & SUNDRIED RATIONALISM
WITH SOME GROUND-UP & ROASTED THINKING
THROWN IN – all shaded brown
like Nescafé – or philosophy – with
similarly pleasant
addictive smells: YOU ARE SUPPOSED TO PICK
                              WHICH BLEND OF GRITS
                              MAKES BEST SENSE
                              FOR YOU TO CHEW:

but Peter doesn't read it. To him, the sign
is a bit of wood squiggled on with crow-droppings.
                There was a crow
                perched above, which flapped off
as he approached – as if something
                had frightened it.
                He does sit,
for a little rest, in the patch of shade
the big board makes   for a few rabbit-
                                        moments
                                        scritch scratch
                                        with a paw
                                        in the earth which
                                        he now
                                        finds no longer
                                        hard-sandy
                                        but damp
                                        & darkish
                                        cow-dung-brown.
Encouraged, moving steadily at a slow lope as if
he is going to no
particular place, & will take days
to get there, he comes, down tors, & round food-bare
                                        rock ledges,
to the grasses of small settled farms. Comfy pigs. Comfy cows.

Value-judgements're swirling, like Either/Or birds
each in their subjectivity's singular colours

over one end of a valley, & down to its grainrich, sunlit floor.

Over furrows & fissures & flaws in the ground,
a dead man comes walking towards him – telling him
it is the South Country. *It is ugly*, the dead man moans;
Peter Henry Lepus sees it as pretty.

2

By a barn
a man with a huge shining face like the moon
& no fur on his head
is washing a pig. Peter Henry
goes closer
to see if it is clement...to ask for direction.

He hears the man muttering, half to himself –
& half to the pig – but crossly – over & over –
HOG WASH! HOG WASH!
His voice – has sticks swishing in it...
as if it is knocking nuts off a tree
or slicing the heads off weeds.
Peter thinks it would be safer
to talk to the pig – so he squeaks – very softly –
as a rabbit kitten would – to it, but the man
hears & answers, with great civility, using some
of the loveliest words

that Peter has ever heard
only he cannot remember them,
that he is cleaning the pig up, to enter it
in a poetry show, that, if it is like last year,
ninety-eight point six per cent – of the
poems in the show will be 'hog' – 'washed to death' –
                    & the other
one point four per cent – diversely – less 'pure' –
                    & he is putting
a real, washed hog in, to show them the difference
*a bit of wormy life makes...*He has the crate ready
to enclose the pig, which he points Peter towards,
inviting him...with one   enormous paw. *There is room*
in it   for more...
Peter doesn't want to be washed with water –
de-furred – & scrubbed till his skin squeaks
like the hog. He thinks the show
must be a bad place to play
if all the other pigs
are as clean & un-fun to play with
as this cold, stopped pig –
        it has been washed
        with very chilled water –
standing stiffly
on the pained ground. He hears his mother's voice in
        his ears –
she is coming from long ago & far away – telling him
what his brave uncle heard, when he

went looking for the remains of Peter's father –
in Farmer McGruber's garden.
The only good rabbit is a dead rabbit,
sings Farmer McGruber.

Antarctica?

On his way – to visit the *Tractatus* –
where he thinks to find a brave bed
of young stout-hearted lettuces,
to fill in the depression in his middle
as well as the grave hole in the afternoon –
Peter Henry Lepus gets lost
in Kant's *Critique of Pure Reason...*
Pictures...of MAN...& a MOUNTAIN...
& later, men – at least two,
& mountains – ditto two. Chinese Edition.
No alphabet. Scuttering over the pages
he is sure his mother would've found
bright & sane as a well-earthed warren,
tunnelled carefully   out of fresh, soft,
dangerously tumbling sand, Peter discovers no carrots.
He cannot find a lettuce anywhere.

Wittgenstein
comes walking towards him
down an iceberg. He is followed
by a crowd of students
who levitate – six inches
above the ice   & higher
than Wittgenstein, though they seem
less solid. More ethereally dressed.

Now advancing, now retreating, they
& their garments
swirl
around Wittgenstein,
in an icy,
avid mist.

Wittgenstein is wearing
an anguished
look of concentration – wall-to-wall pain stretched tight
across his face. Uncaught & not yet clear thoughts
are hiding in his pockets – roosting
just out of range – like wily
feral hens. His stretching ice-stiff fingers,
curling towards them, cup them & become warm as eggs.
He is wearing a snowy, papery cloak
with black signs, that Peter
does not know are German words, pinned
sparingly to it. Peter does not read
put-to-gether-German-alphabet, yet.
The signs translate: *Go*
back. Carrots are
in the world of empirical facts
& growing in the fields of
the live humans
who plant & work them...

YOU ARE IN THE WRONG PLACE

Peter reads the snow
with his nose, for tracks of scents.
He cannot smell his mother; his sisters,
Turvy, Bolter, Scuttle-Butt, & Somersault,
might as well be dead.
Fact: he cannot smell:
his nose is too cold.
He does four or five small
hard pellets   to cover his
embarrassment...which is invisible
to anyone except himself – & also
as a kind of shamefaced test –
because a rabbit that can't defecate
leaving   visible evidence that another rabbit –
if there were any round – could see –
is likely to have transgressed
into death,

& shuffles about a bit
on the white, slippery world –
upon which, mistakenly,
he thinks to sit.

As he slides
lugubriously down
the hard
ice of a floe, killer whales,
with a piteous dinner-longing
on their faces, rise up critically –

lunging – to assess him –

a small –
bite-size –
tear-soggy rabbit, in a blue
snuffle-sodden jacket, not at all
distinguished – here – in his poem of woe.

Ringing in his ears,
as he slides
towards the killer whales
who're now halfoutof the water –
in their paroxysm – to get at him –
the one thing
that Wittgenstein said,
that Peter heard...

(Not
Do not believe   all
of the Tractatus Logico-Philosophicus...

It is our language that determines
our view of reality, because we see through it...
not vice versa...
Go piecemeal, but)
Watch out   for the (written)
intoxication of the mind
& the (spoken)
intoxication of the jaws.

'Calcutta':

French beans think they are on the wrong land mass
& wither into desiccations of homesickness.
Peter Henry Lepus gets lost in 'Calcutta'
on his way to visit Farmer McGruber's vegetable patch.
It is not clement for lettuces in 'Calcutta'
or carrots either. Unfortunately
it is very inclement there
for the famous fat little British rabbit.
He is pursued by hordes, who have
bones poking through the lines of their arms.
Very unfriendly. While running
lappity lappity – rather fast – to get away –
he cannons into the lower portion
of some hard legs hiding under a sari.
When Peter looks up – he sees a warm face
rumpled with brown hillocks & little friendly furrows
like a dug vegetable patch in Farmer McGruber's garden.
Peter *is* pleased to see it – & is 'rescued' –
grabbed by his ears – rather roughly – he feels –
by Mother Teresa, who plonks him sternly
into a liquid-textured *lapin* version
of the miracle of the bread & the fishes.
Peter isn't hungry anymore – & neither
is 'Calcutta'. No one
has camomile tea, after supper. French beans
have finished withering. They are dead. 'Calcutta'
is doing very nicely & thanks you for asking.

Small & Rural

Peter L. is twisting
          this way & that
               time-jumping
in & out   of the texts he is – here – there –
squatting briefly, to sniff the air above,
both   of his ears erect as he listens
to the texts' echoes   getting fainter & fainter
... like a mother's disappearing coo-ee...
Rabbits can hear a car door slam –
     & a favourite text disappearing –
     even from half a paddock away –
     even in 'x' where the word
     paddock   once came from...

     a small field or enclosure, usually a plot
     of pastureland, adjoining a stable...

                              to which
     place   a mother   perhaps may have gone?...

But the word *paddock*   also was used
     to stand for a toad –
     probably   from Old Norse *padda* –
     & for a frog.

Peter doesn't have much time

for frogs, preferring
his own hopping,
but paddocks are all right,
especially if they have grass in them
& the pads & stink
of the dog fox & vixen are absent...

That A Text Should Incorporate
– or try to – Criticisms Of Itself
is a favoured padmark   of all
– & only – the textual foxes.

Ses Arrière-Pensées – A Rueful Survey

Standing (he's
plain as a target)

unguardedly squatting
(with trust!)
on ground where blackberries
creep with stealth

losing his footing
sliding
down hills of obdurate rock

stopping too long
alone in the open
betrayed by the juice of the clover
& the texts of the spring   his mouth
full of grass

what has the rueful
Peter Henry Lepus
to cover his arse?

(More like the stub
of a tale
than A Tale?)

A white fluff powder-puff
– of mingy dimensions – ?

Ephemeral stillness?
A (rabbit's?)
                    dodgy
talent for flitting?
(What use *are*)
Anthropomorphic habits?

What has a fox got
to cover its rear? (in retreat!)
An **ENORM-**
OUS brush! The colour
of marmalade if you
made it from ginger.
Lucent...with rude foxy health.

Peter L. sits kicking at the texts.
He is cross with them

or rather he is cross with himself;
he is kicking – in this instance –
logic texts because *they*
are so unremittingly exact
& *he*
is so unfailingly *errant*...A woman professor
who sat on...committees of rabbits for years...

told him, right at the beginning...

No rabbit's rear

was ever covered by its tail

even in the most

'optimistic'

of the rabbit epics...

Saint Rabbit the Dragonslayer...

or Crusader Rabbit

set in the eleventh century...

Rot from the Head Down?

Later when Peter
tells Russell
how it was – for him –
in Russia – in nineteen ninety-one –
Russell says, It was quite different
– in nineteen-twenty – when he was there;
watch was kept – on visitors – & those they met
& people
'eaves-dropped'
on him & the members of the Labour deputation
with whom he'd gone
to Russia.
Peter wonders
what 'eaves-dropping' is...
His mother has told him
about eaves that hang
out over the edges
of humans' houses –
but those eaves did not
drop off the houses –
Perhaps houses' *rooves* in Russia
fell off on Russell & his friends
wherever they went? Russell shakes his head.
More than once.
It grieves him to think of how
life was – in Russia – then – for Russians. His face

is a field of remembering pain...Middle of the nights
he could hear the sounds
of imprisoned people – being shot –
for being 'idealists'. People he met
were too afraid...of being suspected
of mouthing 'wrong' viewpoints – to try
to hunt – with logic – for any
kind of truth. Everyone was afraid...
as the scaredest rabbit...
of the fox behind the tallest grass...
or lurking...outside the burrow...of who
might be waiting to grab them – for killing –
when they came out.
The four 'most eminent' poets in Russia
were stick-thin, filthy & dressed in rags
when they came to visit Russell
at his hotel. One of them
was allowed – by the Government –
to make his living 'lecturing on rhythmics'.
They kept trying to force him to teach everything
from the point of view of Marx. He told Russell
to save his life he couldn't tell
how the views of Marx came into
beat & stress & the fall
of syllables, nor had
he been able to work out
how   when the ears
hear rain pelting onto a tin roof

they can be taught to recognise
the plonk of a Marxian raindrop
– as distinct – from any other –
in particular – from a Capitalist raindrop.
Russell couldn't help him.

Someone 'high-up' – in the 'equal' government
confided
to Russell, it was felt –

if they could get the near-moribund
necrotic-tissued 'body' of their country working –
by economic theory –
they could put the 'soul' back in
later...
literature, art, music, et cetera

Russell told Peter, about this – as a theory –
in nineteen-twenty he'd had profoundest doubt...

An Art Historian with a Church for a Burrow

Looking for the grass
growing sweetly round the graves
in a forgotten churchyard, in Russia,
in April nineteen ninety-one,
Peter comes to a dilapidated
human work of stone – crammed
with disintegrating ancient books,
one-of-a-kind manuscripts,
& crumbling first editions.
A book louse with her
home under the rubble tells him
once there were one million tomes.
A Russian art historian with a nimbus
rises as if hallowed
above one of the fonts. *We must*
give them back – to the world – he thunders
– from somewhere deep inside his rabbitcoat –
with a fine, ancient, Slavic passion.
He is not talking of 'Hitler's' books – which Peter
is peering at – with interest – but of the
million or so   paintings & other rare
objets d'art, that were 'acquired' – by a strange
troupe of Germans with death
as their end-play
who set up a tyranny – long ago –
to act their death-games out

over as much
as they could manage
of the world.

There is a rat sitting on one of the shelves.
Who is this...Hitler with his name
all over the book-plates?
he squeaks indignantly. *These tomes*
are too old & dusty
to taste good. Some of the paper in them's
over two hundred years old. The ink
gives my children indigestion. In the winters
they smell dank & taste of mould. It is not
a ripe & savoury mould
such as one finds
in the best blue cheeses.
These rank & malodorous books
are a most unsalubrious diet
for a family of elegant rats
whose aristocratic ancestors
once owned a dacha.
                    Had the run of it
for free – more likely, sniffed a sceptic
                              outsider rat
by the door.

          Thickcrusted hunks
of grainy bread, fruit tarts, great wedges of cake –

& Danish cheeses – I would like for my children –
as once I had, the rat rants on stubbornly,
though nobody seems to be listening.

Most of the people
these artefacts belonged to
were murdered, in the ways of the human race
that are most vile, continues the historian.
The thunder in his voice
has moved a little further out.
& is muting itself. A quieter
desperation, instead
behind his tone. *But the owners may have descendants*
or at least...countries...to which
        we could give these stolen world-works back.
        We too stole them when we entered Berlin
as the booty of a war – & we – it is our duty – should
        give them back...though we cannot
raise the dead, to do so – or grant them justice.

Peter's paw goes up to his mouth. His attention
wanders out, beyond the beard & the talk, to a distant
odd & ill-looking tree.
If 'duty' & 'justice' are foods –
& you are hungry for them –
perhaps you should put them inside you?
Grass...belongs to the rabbit that finds it.
Trees...stand...& anyone with teeth

can chew at them. Any bird
with wings & a warning call
can fly to a branch & sing. Ground
belongs to the paws that pad over it
in the moment of passing.
He is not too sure
who owns the rest.
A million things – whether edible
or not – seem too many
for one bearded rabbit to store in its burrow –
or even for a colony with a warren to hold.
Perhaps they could take 'Hitler's' books
& the paintings & chairs – to some big
Village Bazaar, & sell or swap them,
so the rat & his family –
perhaps... his cousins too? – other animals
                    if there were
                    any spare? –
could have good food?
Outside this cold, stone burrow,
there is warm, fine
free sunlight...belonging to any
          body that can feel it...
to which, gratefully, Peter scampers out.

National Shrines (Nobody Wins at a Ritual?)

A long brown nose
reaching out
                    over the wooden
bar of a stall
snuffles softly to Peter:
Hullo friend. They think I am a god
here – on Myashima – but I
was never that. See the necklet of flowers
round my mane & neck? Bowing low,
they bring me rice cakes,
& carrots & apples – at sunset –
& lay them down in little scoops
around my stable door. Sometimes
they pour me sake –
I am getting quite fond of that.
An American poet
came to visit me;
                    he said
his countrymen
did a similar thing,
                    to him –
garlands of purple flowers & votive dishes
of glowing words – all worshipful,
once he was dead.
                    It is most embarrassing
to my horse-nature,

as it was, to his.
He wanted to stay – not being able to worship –
as deeply   he wanted to – all
that his people had made of his homeland...
but some fierce young New Hampshire
women with cameras came clicking this way & scared him...
& he galloped off.
I don't know where he's gone...
They were reading
one of his poems – The Song of the Answerer –
loudly, with ribald snorts. They said he wrote
of a possible Great Poet
always & only as 'he'.
Then they shouted 'Sexist male stallion-shit'.
I don't think he'll be back.

Like the bird-voiced ones, with quieter tread,
that come at dawn & dusk,
they wanted me to bring them
luck – in their lives –
& that – I cannot do.
The gentle ones who bring the flowers
don't seem to hear me when I talk to them.
It is lonely here now Walt Whitman's gone.

Wittgenstein has sped away, to look for Russell,
maybe – in a Hall of a Thousand Mats – built of a single
camphorwood that lost its sap to death four hundred

years ago...or maybe to a temple that is 'keeping safe'
wood that died as a tree in A.D. eight one one...
Peter knows what lonely is – *I can stay*
a little, he whispers
shyly to the horse.
Perhaps, if you have any food to spare,
we could share it?
My legs wobble when I walk.

The straw in the horse's stall
is warm & dry & doze-coloured. After Antarctica
Peter is getting a cold.
        He snuggles down, anxiously
        keeping his eyes open – & his body
well away – from the big horse's hooves
        which look
as if they could come down – on a rabbit's back –
        almost as hard
as one of Mr McGruber's spades – which had
been heard...to split a rabbit in two...
The big horse seems to know.
        I won't move while you're asleep,
        small podgy British visitor,
it blows softly through its nostrils down at Peter,
        huffing chaff at him at the same time,
from the bar where it's resting its nose.
A-choo! Peter has lost the oniony pocket-handkerchief
that he & Cousin Right Way got back

        from Mrs Prickle Sides
        – that his mother gave him – long ago.
                        As he is falling into sleep,
in the dark behind his eyelids,
        the furious haunches
of invisible black rabbits lash out – thudding up
        at him. But the horse
is still.

Circles

When he wakes, Russell is standing over him.
W. & I have argued for three days, he says.
His new work is important, & original –
but I am not at all sure
that it is true. Peter sees the tide has come in –
underneath all the buildings. The shrine
seems to be floating. Russell says it looks
like a mother-duck building, surrounded –
at discrete intervals – by the smaller
wooden ducklings of the lesser shrines.
Peter does not know about that.
He hasn't seen many ducks...
          Once he caught a glimpse
of the Waddle-Splat girls – but they
were upside down in a pond & had
wispy bottoms where their heads should be.
They did, perhaps, look a bit like shrines.
What were their names? Becky?...Jemmy?...
It has got dark. There is no moon.
Wittgenstein has paid   for the priests
to light the stone lanterns in the pine trees
& has taken his shoes off. Peter wonders why
because the ground   is so cold...
Perhaps it is Wittgenstein's bedtime?
W. does not tell him & goes off to look at holes
in the ground in the dark

under trees that are farthest
from the priests' holy glow.
Peter thinks if his mother were out at night,
& so sick she got lost, & their burrow were under
those pines, she would know where to come.
Russell looks out at the lights:
Each one is shut in on itself   like a human being,
he notes. *None of the light circles touch one another.*
At the edges the light   gets gradually darker – ;
it's not clear where light begins & darkness stops.
Wittgenstein   will write about this.

'Japan'

To say 'I have pain' is no more a statement
about a particular person than moaning is.
WITTGENSTEIN, *The Blue Book*

Enormous legs of raddled wood
stand out in water...as if they had
been wading...on some invisible path,
got tired...& stopped & stiffened there...
Maybe they'd been plodding out
towards a pine-furred mountain, that might
have good burrow-holes in it? Peter
would like to get to it. The mountain
is getting its paws wet in a huge water
that Peter, on the other shore,
does not know is sea. He is on a rim
that reeks of what is outside his experience.
Polluted fish are starting to be dried –
their little bodies laid out on the rocks
in absolute surrender – as if they are offering
what's left of themselves up
to whatever gods may be. Nearby
old men with bark-wrinkled faces
are moving their fingers in & out of holes...
as if they were mending...like his mother
used to mend small rabbits' clothes. They seem
to be making the big holes into smaller ones.

Perhaps it is a trap to catch blackbirds
that Peter has seen, once,
flung over parts of a pear tree
near the orchard wall. But where
are blackbirds, pear trees, here?

The shore Peter is on has only small pebbles,
rocks, boats, men – & the strange smells.

Sitting with his head in his hands but still
achingly attached to the rest of him, on one
of the rocks is Wittgenstein. When he lifts
his haggard face, ravaged with self-doubts,
Peter sees he is not feeling well. Shadows
under his eye sockets're shaped like full,
black moons. *You may ride*
to the island on my Notebook, he says, *if you wish,*
only do not misunderstand...Philosophy
is action.

What W. calls his Notebook, Peter cannot see;
he can make out a kind of flat, wooden ferry...
that wasn't there – before Wittgenstein came.
If I could think clearer, today, little rabbit,
I would explain it better.
If I could come with you?
Russell is on the island. I need to explain
in person, the new work, to him.

My words need me   to interpret them   or they
probably won't be understood.

A dangerous delusion, grunts someone
whom Peter – up till now – has not seen –
who is squatting – rude & nameless –
on his haunches   further down
the chill, windless beach. *An author*
cannot count on standing, like a fixture,
behind his or her work, propping
what he or she says
is its meaning up.
Once words are printed
they are texts & anyone can talk to them
as they talk to & amongst themselves. One word
leans backward   taking meaning

from the words behind it...& forward...deferring
its meaning to what comes after it. In fact,

life is one long, different kind of sentence;
the deferrals, there too, are endless, mate.
But as a concept, the author

as chief sauce-tipper   of the tomato sauce
of meaning, is, to put it crudely, somewhat smeared.

Wittgenstein is starting to bang his hands

up & down on the air. He is either trying
to warm them, or he is getting cross. He has
been misunderstood.

Cancer, which has been listening too, beside Peter,
turns its head & walks quietly away. It has decided
to wait for Wittgenstein, somewhere up ahead.

Talk of deferral makes Peter's tummy rumble
like Mt Fuji would – if it were to start up.
He is not about to spit out
volcanic ash & baked rock, but his empty middle
is telling him something simple, about its state.
Perhaps, on the island, there will be food made
that a rabbit...might eat?
Mother-made onion soup? Or a sandy roof
with a string of brown onions hanging down
that a rabbit could stretch to & snitch?

They step   onto the flat float of wood
so loaded with people, that, at its edges,
water is lapping over the planks. Peter
gets his paws wet & when he licks them
they taste not at all...like fur that has
been washed, in a sweet clean rain-drip shower,
in a tub on a burrow's sandy floor
in an age before nuclear waste.

After gliding over a windless expanse
that is smooth & polished
as a grey, silken stone,
after a while the ferry stops
& they clatter & patter off.
When Peter looks back –
at the grey
underwater –
he sees the ferry
has already
slipped down
like a red
autumn leaf
whose season
has gone.

Sun Shadow, Moon Shadow

A Preface?

Peter Henry Lepus is not fond of 'Prefaces'; he says that though they are the 'face' you see before the 'face' of the other writing, he feels they should more properly be called placed-first tail notes, as they are done after the other longer writing.

Peter Henry has one paw resting
on a fat volume of Derrida;
he can't lift it but someone kind
has copied one whole paragraph out
in BIG letters
& pinned it to a broad-trunked tree.
The trunk is covered by the writing
which is on white paper & easy to read.
What it signifies he has no idea
but he likes to run questioningly to & fro
& nibble on a sentence's
'possible meanings'.
Some of it will sink in
in time he thinks...
He is older, now, than he was
when those poems were written.
It is later now than it was then, whenever then was.

Between one line & another there is white

space; between one live trunk & another,
there is an opening...

Peter Meets the American

Peter
            meets the American
critic Altieri
                        sitting
                                    on his squat.
'Whose squat?'   'Get off
your squat,' says Altieri.
                                    'I want to see your
"means of production" – '
Peter
            is not producing
at the moment & doubts
whether Altieri   could see
how he *did it*   were he to hop...
either if he *were*   producing PELLETS FOR CRITICS   then...
or,   if he   were not.   What kind of Marks
does he leave, afterwards? He
has never   gone back to look, preferring
always
to MOVE ON.
He is sitting quietly, now,
in the shadow of a bush,
on a buffalo grass lawn, at Annandale – Altieri
having gone. Peter
is at the Poets' Union
1998 Moon Viewing Party. He has already

sampled their buffalo grass, & decided,
in his forthcoming
Encyclopaedia of Australian Grass Poets,
(& their favourite ROOTS)
to classify it under
EDIBLE BUT TOUGH. He's afraid
what goes under EDIBLE BUT TOUGH
will almost fill the book
which the University-of-
Southern-Queensland-in-Kyoto
has 'scheduled for production' – reluctantly –
in the year two thousand & two.
Peter has heard some talk
about the 'yen' being sick & that, perhaps,
by then, it will have recovered.
He's heard others speculate
that the University-of-Southern-Queensland-in-Kyoto
will gain MORE, from sales of the book
back to AUSTRALIA
if the 'yen' is up...
Peter wonders if the 'yen' is sick,
like those Chinese pandas he met, from not getting enough
to eat, perhaps he should take it some surplus product:
freshly dug carrots, crunch-crisp,
with feathery green tops...
but he cannot find any, not in this
hard-on-your-bottom rainless summer garden. He's overheard
an elderly poet (now ensconced in a chair)

announce that the ground is as hard as a certain
famous ex-politician's thigh muscles.
It was a 'grass roots' politician,
Peter remembers,   in the *SMH*, some
months back...

Most of the poets
are sitting on the grass
without nibbling it.
Mostly they are talking about
what jobs they have – in order
to support themselves
while learning – to write.

THERE ARE NO
AUSTRALIAN GRASS ROOTS POETS AT THIS PARTY
he notes boldly,
in thick black Artline 06 print,
on a little pad
which he keeps
in a hidden
pocket of his fur.
Despite the brave lettering, he is not happy...
or comfortable,
squatting quietly here in the moon shadow, looking up
at the big white Dipper, the alien stars.
But presently his ears prick, he begins to listen.

They are talking
about a writer called 'Marks'
who it seems was interested
like Altieri in 'means of production'.
Since he grew up, Peter has found out
how rabbits
'get produced'; he thinks
he could talk
to 'Marks'
about that.

They

They use a pronoun called I
all the time. It seems to hop around
with them. But you can't see it properly
not all of it. Not like you can see
ears or whiskers,
or paw or a sun shadow.

This is what Peter tells the flowerbed rabbit
who lives deep in dark leaves
that grow straight to a sky of apple-red flowers.
She can't read.
He shows her   the straight line
her paws scraped
on the rained-on damp
green-growing ground: *that's 'I'*; he puts
two short, stiff twigs – one each – same length –
at the line's
head & foot: *that's their*
Capital I.   *But it doesn't* ***MOOOVE***,
she objects: *those twigs, that scrape*
will ***NEVER*** *hop.*
Peter's ears twitch – but he has to agree. Goes on.
Struggles – how   to explain: 'I's written representation'?

It's a picture,
he says at last, *it's a stand-for*

what lives in each of them, it's common
to all of THEM – as the earth beneath our paws
is common to all of us (including them)
who run, hop, walk,
fall, lie, or die on it.
She doesn't know what die is. *It's a word*,
he says, *like I is: nobody knows what it's like*
inside it.
I die, you singular die, he dies, she dies, it dies,
you plural die, we die, they die –

He's given her a lecture
when all he wanted to do
was follow the white
bobs of her tail
disappearing
into the scarlet flowers.

The Hairy Rabbiters

Extract from 'A Perspectived Report on an Australian Menace' (soon to be published by The Asylum of the Rabbit Press):

On the first fleet
were several silverish
grey haired rabbiters.
On arrival they spread quickly.
Like a silver-greyish human blanket
the hairy rabbiters spread across Australia.
Rabbits were distressed.
In the year of the Federation of the Rabbit,
the government gave unprecedented amounts
of electricity, money & fencing materials
to help rabbits build fences
to keep the hairy rabbiters out. But the rabbiters had
sharp teeth
& having bitten through the fences, then used to bite the sheep,
at first eating them raw but later setting bushfires, to barbecue
the sheep in larger numbers, which irritated
the colonial-imperialist
aims of the foxes. Parts of Australia
could never be the same as England
once the rabbiters had arrived.
They were such a pest to the multiplication of sheep
that the Government of New South Wales
gave a bounty of five cents a head
for the scalp of each rabbiter collected.

Children killed rabbiters on their
way to school. Carts pulled by
compliant horses
hauled away the carcasses of the dead rabbiters.
In 1888 there were millions of wild rabbiters in Australia.
Before refrigeration
the red-blooded ones were canned & sent to England as food.
Sometimes cans of these dead rabbiters
exploded in the Red Sea making it
even more red than ketchup
on corpses in Dolby Digital movies.
Thousands of snakes were bred & released in
rabbiter-infested areas, such as deserts & swamps,
But snakes
were not good at catching the rabbiters.
They preferred to hunt & strike
small mammals & birds
which were easier to paralyse & swallow.
The snakes soon grew into huge feral monsters
which terrorised the sheep
by striking them from underneath.
Rabbits have used all kinds of gases & smells
to drive the rabbiters off the continent.
But the rabbiter has never been a lemming.
Rabbits resorted to mixing imported oleander bark
in the rabbiters' beer & billy tea.
But it was a slow way to kill them & innocent
insects, European wasps

& birds drank the lethal billy tea & beer. Today rabbits use
four-wheel-drive vehicles
& hunt the rabbiters with sharp-toothed ankle-traps –
& guns. Trucks with freezers carry the
skinned & dissected rabbiters to market. They
make a tasty delicacy on *table d'hôte* for tourists.
A factory makes thousands of hats from rabbiters' epiderms.
About fifteen rabbiters' skins are needed
to make one Akubra hat.
In recent months a form of AIDS which only affects rabbiters
has been introduced. Rabbits reject this as too brutal.

Picasso's Salad

Picasso at *The Nippy Rabbit*
upstairs, eating Greek Salad, with his daddy,
digging his painterly paws
into the watery oils,
lettuce that pongs of garlic.

His eyeballs protrude
as cones; each
has been drawn
with a conic section.

Methodically his paws
raise to his mouth –
he is eating –
round
black olives,
cubes of ricotta,
rings of glue-pale onion.

Mathematical formulae
boil, out of his eyehalls, & float –
cartoonlike – across
the restaurant's tables.

Picasso's daddy is gazing
at his son & talking

with his mouth full.
        (But there are bushes
        growing over the dad's face.)

Peter is quite bemused
(& distressed)
when he wakes –
the smell of onions
in his nostrils –
he has fallen asleep
on a hessian
bag of them
down
deep
in *The Nippy*
Rabbit's cellar.

What
is he doing there?
Almost
he can remember...
looking up, he sees his paws
have left their dustprints
on the small square
of a now open street-level window
(Peter's dad
never talked
to him

with love & a mouth
full of carrots:
perhaps it was that
he climbed in through?)
& beyond, as if in a time warp,
cubic equations
jumping all around him,
Pablo Picasso, full of Greek Salad,
leaving
The Nippy Rabbit
with his bosky long-dead daddy.

At the Poets' Union Party, June 31st, 2002

On the verandah, a fly-wire door bangs open
interrupting Peter's meditation.
It swings outward, on to the garden,
hitting the wall behind it so hard
it leaves a dint & takes out
several small plaster chunks of the 1980s.

The person who has 'thrust it
forward into the future'
looks thin, brown, & ferocious, but has
a white puffy face
like one of Peter's mother's
just risen
burrow-made scones.
                                        (It is *not* Charles Altieri
Hank Lazer   or anyone Peter knows.)

Pale Poet pushes roughly past,
almost squashing Peter,
heading for the dark at the front of the garden.
It's as if he doesn't know Peter's there.
Perhaps the pasty person's stupid as well as rude
Peter thinks.

Good, says Hank Lazer, who's heard
they're getting a website & has

dropped in...for the views.
An old-fashioned
poetic opening! But different!

If one poet   bangs it shut,
the next one
will open it...

looking for the loo...
or the cold & frosties...

Peter thinks, if Altieri came back,
he could offer *him* a cold & frosty
& Altieri could go & see
how THEY get produced
out of the refrigerator,
which to Peter
is something of a miracle,
though disappointing –
it doesn't
have any of *his* food
but only
the cold & frosties
which he's heard said
are the means
by which
poems
are produced.

Could the refrigerator door
be a poetic opening too?

No poems come singing out of it
while Peter's watching.

Peter's mind is on 'means of production'
but of a more personal kind.

Perhaps 'Marks'
would be a good one to broach it with   since
he's heard 'Marks'
is now living underground, so shares
a common locus
with THE RABBIT.

What he talks
to people about
has become
something of an issue, for Peter, since
he has learnt (better) how to read
& so to talk, standing upright tall
on his two
strong backlegs,
                    almost confident,
                    unless the person
whose knees he's looking up at
has a gun.

'Web'd'

Peter has learnt
about under-determined poetry
from the Canberra poets
by reading one or two
& about OVER-DETERMINED
from some Sydney poets, at whose
websites he has sat,
gazing for hours...they were not
the kind of web sites
he'd come across, before.

The lady orb spider in
Centennial Park
had often let him watch
her woman her web
S
T
R
U
N
G
H
U
G
E

between two conifers,

rippling bushfire red, at sunset,
or lit   by the Sydney summer sun, at noon,

& dotted gaily green
with the iridescent backs
of drained
& waiting to be drained
small to medium-sized
blowflies.

Watching, Peter's seen
the lady orb weaver
closing in,
& snuffled   but not for them

who will never be
any closer
to 'home'
than they are now.

A Sunlit Morning, Labor Day, Late Twentieth Century

Zed is the letter
for the sound the blowfly makes
when it finds his friend the magpie
lying on the grass
head hunched, his black wings
spread fanwise taking sunlight.
He does not sing
though Peter squats beside him, waiting.
His friend's mouth & tongue
are torn & black; old blood
has set & cracked: the flesh
that'd set in jagged peaks
has been re-opened scarlet.
A white ring
jags into the magpie's flesh
at the back of his beak – too hard & stiff
for him to close it. The ring
nooses his head, burying itself
in the neckfeathers' snowcape.
It's shortening his neck. Peter sees
why, yesterday, when he tried,
his friend
couldn't scoop up drink

from the swimming pool, & why
for days, when he flies
he's been dropping the spiders.
Fallen from the branch
where Peter saw him dozing late last night
he does not move when a bark boat
drops from above, so close
it almost hits him.
Squatting beside the magpie's face,
Peter hopes his friend's enjoying a proper
sunlit-morning grass-sleep with no pain,
not merely hurting with his eyes shut.
When he hears the girl from WIRES say
to the mobile,
It was too late – he is surprised. WHAT
is 'too late'?
It is late but not 'too late'
for the girl from WIRES to get some scissors
from her handbag
& insert them between
the serrated white two-litre-milk sealing-ring,
& his friend's snowy neckfeathers
& set him free
so that, when he wakes, he can stretch his neck.
It is late – but not 'too late' –

to fly a food-load up to that Sydney bluegum
where his friend's youngest offspring,
a bug-eyed baby grey, unable to fly,
with bones showing close to the skin
like bones Peter's seen
in photos of humans in Belsen,
waits stuck screaming on the nest rim.

Laws

I

If
you were hoping
this or any
poem
was going to leap up
off its page
& absolve you
from the critical
necessity
of having
to work out
how to live
your life
for yourself
you were **wrong.**

Laws

2

Humans
rank their species
above – & prefer it to –
any other, Peter says. *For a geneticist,*
there is no rational basis   for elevating
one species   above   any other. Peter
has been told this
by a man who once
wrote a preface to a
book by Richard Dawkins,
& now, having found
some lettuces
                    that humans left   going to seed
all by themselves, in the middle of a field, halfway
up a steep hill, where there's been
some fallout
of plutonium dust, with a resting mind
& a soothed & busily digesting gut,
he wonders WHY   humans   like humans best?
It is natural – for a rabbit – to like lettuces
better than OTHER RABBITS   *most* of the time –
but Peter 'knows'   he has been   'removed'
                                                            from *some*
of the lores
          of rabbits...has left...his native land, his

narrative, his text...

what's more, has

no rabbit's foot

to touch

except his own – & so, he likes (mildly)
his family & his e x t e n d e d f a m i l y –
whisker-wobbling & jittering down holes
at NOISES OF NEIGHBOURS Who *wouldn't*
be rabbit, & get in a funk sharing digs
next to ferret, bigoted human, dingo, or fox?

'Moonlight Becomes You'?:

'Indeed it does' purrs Chairman Miaow
from his poised pose
on the wickerwork chaise-longue,
on the verandah, in the moonlight.
He is recumbent
by
an as yet unopened sardine can.

He is CAT who is white
as the moon is white. As hunger grows,
he lashes his tail. But quietly. His eyes
watch the can as if it is a work of art.
He is a white cat
but empty.
The moon is full.
The small sealed can gleams seductively.
He is intrigued
by the cunning
art of its closure. Dropping
from the chaise-longue
onto the verandah, whiskers low,
he begins to sniff around the sardine tin,
testing it, occasionally giving it
a little tough buffet, or a velvety swipe,
with one of his moon-silvered claws.
His eyes too perhaps

gleam with the cunning of his makers;
natura morta, his feral mother –
large she was & squat; his father

pure white, though stiff
still stalks with a martial savoir
befitting
a serial mouse-killer.

Unbothered by an absence of mother,
Chairman Miaow *purrrrrs* to the sardines.
                                        Perhaps he is trying
to lure them to come out,   & dance *inside him*
in the moonlight?

Peter is quite depressed
& crouches even lower.
He has chosen to hide under rose bushes.
New. Pruned. Their leafless canes
don't make a shadow
                                        that would hide him
from the Chairman.

Matisse who travelled
between cultures also
found no rules
for art   outside the self,

but to have
or to share
this personal finding
he needed the art
of a language
that devolved

from many
selves...their
cognitions...& recognitions...

Peter at this moment
would rather live by guile
than die by art.

He wonders if the sardines
got into the can alive

& what it would be like
to die there...

What it would be like
to...die...inside the Chairman

... is there moonlight?...

New Poems

In 'the Ukraine'

He meets a man with an icicle voice
who says it is 'Mind's disease'
to act impulsively; this man elevates
'Reason' to a pedestal, where he worships
at a cold, stony chiselled face, from afar
(& sometimes Peter sees him go up close, to peer,
at something old, cold, & slushy, underneath it –
which, he tells Peter, is a high I.Q.-ed
pickled brain, in a jar).
The cold man reads Peter, from his big,
darkblue worn-covered book, about the name 'Peter'.
Peter knows names are second-hand & jump
onto a rabbit's back while she or he is asleep;
that rabbits wake up wearing names
they think are their own. He
doesn't want anything to do
with some
of the people who've worn his
name before...that one back in the
dark hole of time gone backwards...
twelfth-
century Latin, *Petrus*, the book says, means 'stone'
& the other, earlier one,...who gave the name
to a man called Simon, who then probably was
called that – even by his mother –
did she have to put 'Saint' in front of 'Peter'
as the book says, even when she scolded him...

or when she told him to learn the list of DON'Ts?
When the man tells Peter
some of the other meanings – behind his name –
Peter guesses why   that one jumped onto him:
to run out   as a stream
or vein of ore   peters out; to fail,
die out, disappear... Peter knows
all about disappearing... Right now,
                                        doing a bolt
                                        down a burrow,
to get away from the cold man. Suddenly the burrow opens:
blue skies, pale-green ears of wheat,
wavering above him, a small green patch, late sown,
beyond it, brown.
As he scrambles out, up through
the wheat roots he nibbles
a few whitish below-earth stems – in passing
just to test.
        Now, either on fours or standing,
he cannot see over the wheat. The ground
under his paws feels flat. There is wheat
in every direction. Singing
voices he hears & the earth vibrates
with the trundling sounds of cart wheels.
He hops tentatively
towards the sounds of the voices...
It is eleven years to the year two thousand
in the Ukraine...Singing & dancing humans
are bringing in the wheat.

A girl tells Peter:
We have done this for hundreds of years.
Next year we
will not plant wheat, & we
will not eat this harvest.
We are one hundred & sixty k.
north of Chernobyl: this wheat
is death.

Between what you see
& what you say...
there is always difference; the wheat
looks beautiful & Peter
has eaten some...
His body the house
of the unprovable link?
Peter goes, with the girl,
to visit her sister
who lives in a hospital
of tired little children
whose bodies hurt
when they are awake
& when they are asleep; *My little sister*
is not getting better, the girl murmurs so softly
Peter almost cannot hear.
Outside high brown ears of wheat
wave & ripple under blue skies
wide as those over desert – Peter's eyes
cannot see an end to it.

Ideations?

Peter has seen
a MAP OF THE WORLD
in an atlas once,
when he was very small.
There were
lots of coloured shapes,
which his youngest sister Bolter said
had the names
of 'countries'
printed on them;
around the coloured shapes
there was much blue. He'd not known, then,
that the colour blue was used for water,
nor what the words 'Atlantic'
or 'Pacific' named.

Bolter had not told him
what the word
                    'country'
meant,
          then...
                    to her...

He thinks of the many
coloured shapes
he's flown across,

the ups & downs –
& grasses –
of grounds
on which he's hopped,

the texts
he's read,
fallen into,
& out of,

to get back
to where
he is now.

He's still not sure
what humans mean

when they talk
        about
'The World'.

The Batless Sky

The villagers used to squat
beating drums all day
under their trees, to keep
bats from settling, eating fruit
that the villagers sold for income;

he has a long memory
of using sodium arsenate
as a weedkiller, when working
a rubber plantation for an
absent corporation in Malaysia,
this Brit who claims he is seventy-eight
tells the mad Dutchman
who claims ***he*** is over eighty.
                                        To Peter
they sound as if they're
competing
to win the prize
of who's the elder.
They have been discussing the use
of pesticides, fertilisers, & weedkillers,
by market gardeners round Sydney
who can't read,
& who
identify
the pesticides

by smelling them
in the bottle.
Peter
is lurking under a park bench
bored. He wishes they would get back
to talking about the fruit bats.
We used sodium arsenate
because it was cheap. I used to mix it
& spray with it. ***I didn't***
die of arsenic poisoning.
You were 'working manager'?
interposes the Dutchman. The Brit's
short outburst in Malay deliberately excludes him.
What about the spray that went into the ground,
what did that kill? Peter wonders. *What about the lizards*
that crawled under the baby rubber plants
around which the Brit had been spraying
to take out the smotherlove of the weeds...
how did they like
the earth they lived on –
over which ants
& other small lives
also walked –
being misted & dripped upon
by arsenic?

He has been to visit, recently,
a Science graduate 'organic' market gardener

whose discourse was full
of the 'dangers to product', of the 'indiscriminate
use of chemicals'. Also, (she mentioned)
the fallout on fauna...

We used to employ children, too.
The village children used to come & ask for work.
We paid them for weeding
where we didn't want to spray. Nobody
in that village was starving. They came
because they liked
the 'status' of having a job...identity
... it wasn't just money...

All this talk about money, Peter mutters,
why don't they talk more
about where the bats have gone? He is gazing up
at the grey near-rainy sky; a few
currawongs have crossed it, stroking strongly
to reach their roosting places, but, as yet,
no bats have swooped in disagreeing over foliage-holds,
chittering in dusk trees full of possible
bat-landing positions.
A week ago he heard the Dutchman & the Brit
arguing about something they heard on the radio
half-hearing, each in their different rooms
at opposite ends of inner Sydney,
the same news bite: *The Royal Botanical Gardens*

decision to cull...the bat population...
reluctant...damage to rare...trees & shrubs...

Peter has looked up 'cull' in a dictionary:
'reduce the population of (an animal)
by selective killing'. In his experience
humans use the word, also, euphemistically:
it can mean 'exterminate' one kind of life
in the region the cullers are working in **TOTALLY**.
His whole being is feeling the big
absence of the bats, who were part
of his experience of
the nightsky of Sydney.

What about the bats' absence from their lives?
the Flowerbed Rabbit asks him sharply.
All you are thinking about
is how **you** *are feeling. What*
are you going to do
for them, who have, if what you suspect
is true, no lives to make their
nasty noises in? The Flowerbed Rabbit
doesn't really like the bats,
their arguments frighten her – as much
as those of humans; she can't sympathize with the hours Peter
spends gazing up, watching them swing, chittering bat-talk
incomprehensible as English, Greek and Urdu to a non-native
speaker; he tells her

he is trying
to learn what the sounds mean by studying
how bats use them. *Why?* she asks him, he thinks, brutally.
Some things are...beneath
&...below...words, is all
he can answer her. A deep breath. ***I am trying***
to study EVERYTHING.

This Aggression...

This aggression is addressing us,
Peter Henry informs the Flowerbed Rabbit
who doesn't need to be informed,
who's squatting beside him. Peter Henry
is testing two new words he's learned;
with his eyes very still, & wide,
he is gazing at her
to see if she's impressed. It's hard to know.
They are being harangued in the park
by a septuagenarian Dutchman. Who tells:
I woss in Java...during war. I woss
in prisin camp...the Japanese...
The more he talks the louder it gets.
He's swinging his arms,
boot-stamping,
jumping about.
Despite being almost eighty
he's dangerous,
moving fierce as a Heteropoda Huntsman
that's had its prey removed. The Flowerbed Rabbit,
flinching, has turned her head away.
Her ears point longingly towards
the flowerbed's clump
of sawtooth-jagged fern,
but Peter signs her PLEASE
not, just yet, to go.

He wants to know what the strange rasp
voice might say. He's never heard a human
rage this way before.
I woss a boy, my family poor
bit I talk...good Dutch, I go good school
later when I go Holland people say
you must be very important you talk Dutch so good
why you dress poor?...In Holland, people dumb,
he snorts with scorn.
In Java, Jewish people in camp,
the Dutchman spits, *they tell Japanese*
who has gold...the Japanese take those people
beat them torture to make tell where gold...
If gold, they kill't.
If no gold...they kill't anyway...Jews not tell
on Jewish people...only on others in camp,
the Dutchman roars, *I boy   in camp   we starve.*
His ancient muscles bulge like hawthorn stones.
He brandishes the big brown stick
he walks with high, hitting
at unseen heads in the air. One end
of the stick has a small round knob
that he holds. The sharp steel spike at its other end
makes Peter's ears twitch anxiously. He hops two big
human paces back. The Flowerbed Rabbit's bolted
several stick-whirls ago. Peter can see
only her unmoving eartips, above the nearest sawtooth fern.
The Dutchman is left ranting to clouds,

even the patientest pigeons have gone.
Eventually he slows down, reverts
to collecting the metal cans for scrap,
dropping them into hessian bags.

Relativities

British beekeepers benefit from global warming, Peter hears
some poet say; his ears
point tall in surprise, he thought
bees kept themselves, he's often seen them
flitting through tea-tree scrubs
that overhang,
from one bank of the Goodradigbee
to the other,
above the widening ripples
from the fallen beetles
the rising mouths of the trout,
& it did not seem
to him, then, that any ONE
was keeping those bees
from buzzing exactly where they wanted to...

Since the British
foot-&-mouth cull,
there are three million less
plant-chewing mouths, to eat the summer wildflowers
in the British fields, the poet continues;
it will be a good summer
for the British beekeeper.

Peter's eyes grow round with envy; he too
would like to see again,

those fields...full of summer grasses...
his distant relation, Picasso Rabbit,
has emailed him of the rhapsodic taste
of a glass of liquid grass, that a
man called away by mobile phone
abandoned undrunk
on a rabbit-high bench
outside the Cromwell Road branch
of mega-store Sainsbury's;

Picasso claimed the juice
produced at Sainsbury's,
in a bar called CRUSSH,
at the spelling of which
Peter's nose wrinkled dubiously, tasted far superior
to any grass
from the poet-trampled grounds of the Lake District.

The email about the grass (coupled with
the poet's talk of June fields)
has planted in Peter an urge
to stow away
on a Grass-Sampling Tour
of England & Ireland. Since his return from Dili, Fiji, &
Yogyakarta,
having stowed away to Guthega, chilled in the boot of
of someone's rear-rust-holed car, he has seen June snow
on New South Wales's

Snowy Mountains; he has been too long
in warm places, he thinks,
noticing
his fur grown summer-thin,
to like
sleeping burrowless
in the Sydney parks, at seven degrees,
with the lightly-clad homeless humans
& the better-furred possums.

Peter Henry Lepus in 'Iraq, 2003'

Far from the Shatt al-Arab

Peter wonders if pigs could fly
& thinks, yes, they could, pink & squealing,
if someone put them in a helicopter.
He doesn't know   it's **NOT**
'all right'   to fly around
with **PIGS** in a Muslim country.
He's heard planes overhead all day –
he's somewhere on the outskirts
of Baghdad – there is, it seems,
some kind of 'war' going on.
What is 'war'? He hears the Flowerbed Rabbit's
anxious voice in his ears, though she is far away –
something she'd wanted to understand, when they
were sampling fresh ears of seeding grass,
after the two thousand & two
Australian drought'd turned
parts of western New South Wales
into desert; other parts of Australia, too,
he'd mused, then; they'd been out west,
wild pigs around...
                    the seeding grass
'd come **after** the rains...
                    Where is rain, **now**,
in this Iraqi desert?
He couldn't answer the Flowerbed Rabbit.
He'd arrived in Fiji after the coup...

& anyway, that wasn't a 'war'.

He is drifting into sleep, without shelter,
                                        on the flat
dry gritty sand that's plainly not
greybrown like rabbit's fur – he's aware
of nowhere to hide...Dreaming of Arctic
animals whose fur
's mistakenly stayed dark
when the first, Arctic snows came down,
he sees, on the sand,
the small troubled figure
of the philosopher Alfred Jules Ayer
crouched under a rock. There is a
scratched drawing of a tree
with the letters 'Bo'
scrawled under it.
The philosopher's paws are clasped
round the pages of a book
with LANGUAGE, TRUTH, AND LOGIC
emblazoned on its spine.
It seems he is struggling with RE-
VISIONS to this work
which he first finished
                                        in n i n e t e e n
            t h i r t y-
f i v e.

Putting out a shaking paw, Ayer says, in less
than confident 'voice', *I am gaining a sense-datum*
of fur, long ears, & round, brown eyes,
the sense-experience of what
in language, I'd likely call a rabbit.
Ayer cogitates. (Has
his remark, his 'locutionary act',
given the impression
he is 'impulsive', 'hasty', 'rash'?)

Peter thinks about the Flowerbed Rabbit's head.
He can imagine her plunging headlong
down a burrow. When she's scared, it's what
he's sometimes seen her do.

Ayer worries. He thinks he's been accused,
by another philosopher, of making
'**too headlong**
expositions'...(Were John Langshaw Austin's
counter-arguments
right?)
He has, he says, been teasing out
his most famous book's
arguments,
& themes – perception...knowledge of 'the past'...
knowledge of 'other minds'...for most of his life.

Peter's ears turn

to catch every bit of what Ayer is saying.
He asks, *What*
is your most famous argument about?

Ayer has been eating dates.
Dried-out stones, bone pale & sticky, strips of the darker
date-flesh clinging to them, rest on the sand.
He has placed *Language, Truth and Logic* at his feet.
He does not speak. He is remembering finishing
A Concept of a Person and Other Essays,
which Macmillan, London, published
in nineteen sixty-three.

Peter is remembering the Tigris & Euphrates,
how he
threaded his way through some marshes
to get to where he is now.
He has been reading *The Middle East Review*, & realises, he is
now south-west of Baghdad – a long way north of
Shatt al-Arab, where the two rivers have one mouth.

He remembers seeing
estuarine wildlife die, after the oil spills
during the Gulf War. He was in Kuwait, then.
He also remembers the fires. He did not see the war.

The sky is black from smoke plumes somewhere beyond them.
Parts of Baghdad seem to be burning.

Ayer is muttering about his 'criteria of verifiability'.
Austin seems to think he got it wrong.
Peter says, *Parts of Baghdad are on fire.*

* * *

The Kurds need a state of their own, Ayer says.
Peter looks at the newspaper in Ayer's shaky grip.
It is one of Rupert Murdoch's. It affirms:
STATELESS KURDS
NEED HOME.

Peter thinks of the pictures of mountains he has seen on the map, to the north, pale brown, a lightish tan...once part of the Ottoman Empire...
Perhaps that coloured place with the 'three thousand metres' mark is where the Kurdish people want their homeland...
He's heard
they've wanted one, for over eighty years.

A little round to the side of the rock,
Professor J.L. Austin is not thinking about the Kurds.

Austin thinks about all the ink he has spent, examining Ayer's exposition of the argument from Illusion.

Was it a WASTE?

Austin is a Professor of Moral Philosophy.
He believes in fine discriminations in the use of words.

He has been thinking all night, re-creating
the argument of a paper
he wrote in nineteen fifty-eight –
Austin is very precise.
His nineteen fifty-eight paper
is about 'action'.
He does not show it to Peter. What he is holding in his hands
has printed on it: **THREE WAYS OF SPILLING INK.**

Peter thinks there might be four ways – if you splashed it
north, south, west, & east. He thinks of the map of Iraq.

The Kurds want an independent state ***to the north***, Ayer says.

Peter hasn't met any Kurds yet.
His tummy is rumbling.
Perhaps there will be grass, dry or dying,
away from Ayer.
He hops closer to the base of the rock, exploring, moving
around it. It is very large, & seems to have some carving –
strange faces, lumpy raised & sunken bits that look like words.
It reminds him of the languages he couldn't read on the Iranian
stones.
Professor J.L. Austin is peering at the carvings.
Peter has seen him before – in a photo

on a desk at Oxford. He remembers reading:
'Professor J.L. Austin...worked in Military
Intelligence
during the Second World War.'
Austin is looking at the vertical lines on the rock, imagining
how something
might flow down them, & how one would,
or might,
describe it.

On the Outskirts of 'War'?

Plink! Plink! Polluted water drips from a rusty pipe
onto something in a dark corner.
Peter wakes to this sound.
He remembers entering the city,
seeing a construction, a building
Picasso-cream, & tall,
with a rounded top
like an onion.
It is plainly not a mosque.
He has seen human sacred sites before.
Part of this building's side has been torn away.
It is like a big burrow open to the moonlight.
He remembers going inside...

It is where he is now. There is nothing to eat.
No sacks of potatoes or vegetables.
The earth smells mouldy; there is a glint of light
near where the water pools & spills,
but nothing grows.
To his right,
above a date palm with half its top blown off
he sees two tiny points of light.
Against the wall that's closest to the moon
there's the outline of a man.
A voice questions softly:
Joshua, why don't you try & find them?
Why are you still here?

The voice seems to be talking to itself.
Peter Henry Lepus can see no other human there.
He listens. It seems the man has built
the house for his fifteen wives, that he is one
of the over-five-million
believers in
the Church of Jesus Christ
of the Latter-day Saints,
who are scattered throughout the world.
His wives scattered out through Baghdad,
leaving him behind
when the bombs began to fall.
They are all called 'Smith', like him
& they came, with him, to this place.
Each one
had a separate
apartment, within the rounded building, so he did not know
till he went to find
one, & then another...& another...
that, finally, he was all alone.

His voice goes back, he is reminiscing
as Peter has heard
Ayer do.

He had left Ayer in the desert, with a group
of hiking phenomenalist philosophers,
each trying to receive a 'sense-datum'
of a big pool of water, that, Ayer said,

wasn't really there. This had puzzled Peter.

He had thought,
when you hopped towards water,
you could drink it.
After rain, it was what he'd seen
the outback wallabies do.

Ayer'd said:
gaining a sense-impression of seeing water
was an 'optical illusion'
that people in deserts sometimes had.
It happened on hot days
when the sun was shimmering on the sand.
He has described groups of people, in desert,
who think they are seeing water,
& there is no water there;
they are correct
in perceiving something,
but deluded
in what they think it is...
Peter'd hoped they were carrying
big pouches of water with them.
He has not seen Ayer since...

The soft voice in the dark space
is still talking to itself: *Joshua, are you*
being punished
for having fifteen wives?

Or, for building this big house
with the top windows shaped like onions?

He'd not wanted a house for them
that looked like the others around it –
houses, mostly, of Arabs,
who went to mosques to pray.

Had he built a needle spire on top
it might have looked
like a Mormon church.
They'd not wanted
to draw...
such false attention...to themselves...
in Baghdad, while they stayed...

yet needed a cool house, for a hot place.

The pale, whitish-green-tinted window-glass
was anti-glare, locally made...

He'd planned
the high dome roof,
to span an unused sunless room, & give them cool
beneath it – the windows,
to catch the breeze.

The onion...a simple food object...
How could it

've cost so much –
few labour-intensive lead strips (unlike stained glass)
the design
mostly done in weatherproof paint?

Coming in, Peter'd noted
the small 'onions' inside the bigger one,
& puzzled about them.
In the past, he's not
been overly fond
of onions. He is trying
to overcome
his dislike...

From the outside,
he'd seen fine lines in a deeper green
curving up each small 'onion', to the top
where there was a slim
darker green stalk.
It's the memory of the smell that makes him tremble.
These 'onions' have no smell.

He's been reading his book
on the 'Philosophy of the East',
& wonders if Joshua knows
in some accounts of Daoism (& Buddhism)
the onion's used as a m e t a p h o r
for the i n s u b s t a n t i a l i t y

of human bodies...

Joshua has begun rummaging,
making paper rustling sounds, looking for his passport
& those of his fifteen wives. They did not
take their passports with them, he discovers,
pulling one passport after another
out of a slim black case.
He has travelled with his wives 'disguised'
as 'sisters', out of Utah.
At first, the sixteen Smiths'd been looking for the place
where 'the Bible's Abraham' had lived.
Peter remembers the 'cradle of civilization',
ancient Mesopotamia,
's been linked to the 'Garden of Eden' myth,
& that the name, 'Abraham',
was connected to this site. Peter, who has been studying widely,
is in Baghdad to collect data
for a rabbit *History of Philosophers*, though he has not,
yet, received authorisation, from Cambridge University,
for his proposed 'research',
nor reached Baghdad University, to do it...
due to 'war'...
Was Abraham a philosopher? he asks Joshua, eagerly. Joshua
does not seem to hear.
He had two wives, he murmurs,
so, there is a precedent
for plural marriage...

It seems the sixteen Smiths

've also been searching for
'The Divine Authorisation'
inscribed on two golden plates.

There were other authorisations, Joshua mutters,
given to Isaac, Jacob, Moses, David, & Solomon.
Perhaps he is secretly hoping
to find some reference
to the Joshua Smiths?...

Peter thinks Joshua's US leave-taking
was, perhaps, a trifle late.
He's read, on the official website
of the Church of Jesus Christ
of the Latter-day Saints,
that it is **o n e h u n d r e d**
& t h i r t e e n y e a r s
since President Wilford Woodruff
advised that the practice of plural marriage
should cease...
furthermore, that in nineteen ninety-eight,
Joshua would likely have been
excommunicated from the Mormon Church,
& in violation of the 'civil law'
of the United States, a virtual outlaw, had he stayed.

Peter has looked up 'mirage'
since he left Ayer. He wonders if the plates

might be some kind of 'mind's illusion',
shimmering gold in humans' heads,
comparable, perhaps   to...
creating 'illusory water' for them,
as the sun seems to,
shining shiftily
in desert,
on sand?

Outside in the moonlight, he can see the bats,
swooping out of what's left of the date palm's crown.
Though,
from where he squats,
on the uneven floor,
he cannot see
the small high 'onion' windows, he suspects
the bats are flitting in & out up there.
They do not look at all
like the Sydney fruit bats he has watched.
He has read, in *Bats of the World*,
... some bats eat fish, birds, other bats...
or frogs. Perhaps these Baghdad bats
are catching moths? They do not tell. They make no sound.
All Peter can hear is the quiet voice of Joshua Smith
telling himself, in bits,
the 'story' of how he came to be
where he is now.

Joshua has always believed the plates are real,
that they contain
the prophecy of a 'primitive American',
named 'Mormon', who buried them
at Palmyra, in New York state, in A.D.
eight hundred & twenty-seven –
a thousand years before
Joseph Smith
dug them out;
Joseph Smith
was led to them
'by revelation'. It's rumoured
the plates, which've been...in hiding...
for one hundred & seventy-odd years
have, comparatively recently,
been re-discovered
under the bomb-crumbles
of Baghdad.

Joseph Smith, it seems,
was the only human
who had
'insider' knowledge
of the one-thousand-year-dead
language, &, so,
was uniquely able
to 'translate'
'Mormon's words',

from the plates into plain
nineteenth-century
'American English'.

Is a language
known only to one person
a language at all?;
                    Peter remembers
Wittgenstein, pacing restlessly
in his study at Cambridge, asking
for clarifying objections,
counter-arguments, from his students.
He feels sure
Wittgenstein would say
that it was not.

Joshua has one date,
left, to eat.
He eats it.
He believes in 'the simple life'.
Abruptly he heads off, barefoot, into the
now day-lit Baghdad streets, to look for any
of his fifteen wives.

Peter wanders off, stopping, to sniff
at empty doorways – the 'burrow' leads back
to Joshua's many-roomed, main house. All
the kitchen cupboards are open,

with nothing inside. He hopes
Joshua will return
perhaps with some spare
ears of wild green barley – or carrots...
He is dreaming
of eating autumn grass
with the Flowerbed Rabbit
when he falls asleep.

A Sack

When Peter wakes, it is night again.
Joshua has returned. There's a radio
& a full sack of barley
on the floor. Josh says he found both
in a house where there'd been fighting.
He has walked & walked.
He has not found his wives.
Peter hops towards the barley sack.
It is very dark where it is on the floor.
He finds the end that's open
& begins, quietly, to chew.
The radio is playing news:
Peter hears John Howard's
unexcited voice announce:
the FA-18 Hornets
have returned to Darwin.
There will be parades
in the Australian cities...
for those returned
from the Iraq War.

It is May fifteen, two thousand & three,
Joshua says.
He continues more softly, *the War has ended,*
but these streets
are occupied by people warring

for the food & water to live on,
or for things to trade,
or sell, for profit.
Around five point three million people
lived in Baghdad, before the war. Now, who knows?
Is it possible
to find fifteen people – among so many –
where it is dangerous to move about on foot;
no public transport, or City Hall,
gangs of shooters, & looters,
& a lot of city to comb. Where might his wives
have gone? Where could they go?
He is determined
to keep trying to find them.
Peter in a corner is digesting barley
& pondering how *he*
might get to Baghdad University.
Joshua begins to build a fire, to boil some water
for drinking, & later, to cook...

Journeys West of 'War'

I Wind on Fencing Wire

Where is he? Peter Henry Lepus wonders.
He is squatting – well past sunset –
in one of the few
mapped
        depressions
in Iraq's Western Desert,
ears turned to one side,
listening to the 'Wind on Fencing Wire'.
Its whistly noises seem to come from somewhere near.
He's heard this CD played before
when he was chewing creek-side grass that grew
– hard, tough, & slightly sour –
near a roadworkers' camp at Oodnadatta.
He remembers a composer from Western Australia
who worked with 'natural sounds'
& a tape recorder.

Coming through strange cracklings
& noises of static
like those emitted
by Josh Smith's
radio
in Baghdad,
he hears an alien voice
speculate:

Maybe it's the wind
that played on the Rabbit-Proof Fence
in 'Australia...del Espiritu Santo'?

Who is listening?
Is it Professor Ayer, he thinks, or *could it*
be Joshua Smith?

He'd left Joshua Smith
walking the Baghdad streets, dodging car bombs,
looking for his wives,
& travelled, mostly at night,
eventually hitching a ride
with a scrawny desert-bound camel
– 'strayed' – it'd said,
from one of the city's bazaars, where
being long unsold, it had suspected
its merchant was going to kill it.
Too skinny to fetch a good price I am,
it'd snorted noisily, then had harrumphed,
Thin camels get eaten in Baghdad.
Peter had not enjoyed the ride.
Its back is not easy to sit on, he'd concluded.
Had been glad to leap off when the camel bent legs
& collapsed to rest on the riverbed at sunset.

Peter's looking for Professor Alfred Jules Ayer
& a group of British

phenomenalist philosophers, who wish
to discuss
the professor's work,
                & to experience
the desert's mirages.
Ayer is observing the behaviour
of wind, sun, & sand.
When Peter last saw him.
Professor Ayer was on a camel heading east,
the pursuing philosophers
far behind him.
They seemed to march as a group, their faces
red, their legs, red, too.
A few, Peter saw, had blisters,
sun-dried, gummed with sand.
Some legs looked very white
where the socks had fallen down.
Peter's camel had not been impressed,
nor wanted to go any closer.
It'd harrumphed again, which Peter
had learnt, by this time, was a sign of
displeasure. He'd been disappointed.
He wants to gain answers to his questions
about the roles
the words
        'language'
                'truth'
                        & 'logic'

have played
in Professor Ayer's life.
Peter's found an abandoned philosophy notebook,
with some writings about 'Illusion'.
                    Working his way round boulders
& up the bank, cautiously he stops,
ears lowered & flattened,
to observe, keeping as close as possible to the ground.
There is someone sitting, knees crossed,
with a camera round his neck. The 'Wind on Fencing Wire''s
being twanged across the desert
from a radio beside a bed roll & a pack.
This person is talking into a little machine
with an aerial, positioned on a plastic sack,
beside a baby-carrots' can, which Peter, inching
towards, sees is empty.

The man, Max Strang, is testing a mobile phone,
which he's just acquired, he says,
from one of the 'post-Saddam entrepreneurs'.

Yeah, there've been more bombs, one near the airport,
there's trouble getting round, street sniping
still going on – some Yanks got shot.
The voice sounds like one Peter's heard before
on Sydney radio, talking from Iraq.
It's in mid-flow...
He's had no real scoops to send, before, or after, the war,

failed to get himself embedded, with the Coalition forces
or with the Yanks; the local TV
won't use him, his Arabic's not good –
besides, it's the wrong kind,
not Formal, literate, written...
but street speech
he's picked up outside Iraq. He's come to the desert
to tape the nocturnal hyenas.
Thinks he might sell
some Iraqi 'natural sound'
to a friend who's a muso
at Griffith, just moved from Woy Woy,
near where
Spike Milligan used to live. If that doesn't work,
he's heard a rumour about some gold...
& a man who's lost a lot of wives...

He is talking to someone called 'Weasel' Smith,
who writes under the pseudonym 'Botany' Jones.
Peter,
who had uncomfortable memories
associated with the English rural weasel,
begins to twitch,
anticipating mention of
their custom
of 'eating rabbit'. He watches
Max Strang's mouth & throat, trying
to forget weasels,

& their larger cousins, the stoats,
&, to remember,
he, Peter Henry Lepus, squats,
as a scribe,
in a different country,
having travelled
into another time, as well as text.

He thinks of his *Rabbit History of Philosophers*,
of where to begin it,
whether with Zarathustra, in Persia,
(six twenty-eight to five thirty-one B.C.) or with
the one called Thales, who's said
to have travelled to 'Babylon', which
Peter's read, lies south of Baghdad,
& of what the Flowerbed Rabbit would say...
Wherever she is, he cannot reach her from here.
Dejectedly, he begins to listen to Max Strang
angrily informing Weasel Smith

about his failed feature story – on how
half a million Iraqi children under five
are estimated to have died
between nineteen hundred & ninety,
when the UN trade sanctions were imposed,
& nineteen hundred & ninety-eight,

as a result of poor health of mothers,

the more general
collapse of health services,
& the lack of power
for the country's water supply
– an ongoing problem –. He castigates editors.
Weasel Smith cuts in, very loudly, *one dead Aussie now – with a*
good shot – taken alive & smiling, in Iraq –
that might make the news.

Max Strang begins to run his fingers
through his greasy hair & talk about
how long it is since he's been under a shower.
He's decided.
He doesn't want to *make the news* anymore.

Over his shoulder, clinging to the strap of his camera,
Peter sees a tiny form emerge.
It has eight thin legs & looks like a baby Huntsman Spider.
I'm Clifta Webb, it says.
Do you know the way to Persia?
It is wearing tiny red cargo pants, over its four
lower legs, the 'waist' ending only part way up
a small, distended, glistening abdomen.
You could go down the Shatt al-Arab,
Peter says, thinking fast.
Why do you want to go to Persia?

Though, on the map, Iraq & Iran nestle together,

he does not think so tiny a creature as this junior spider
could travel, by land, so far, directly east,
walking on those short eight legs –
perhaps even through the dangers of Central Baghdad...

Perhaps you could drop yourself onto a boat;
you would need to travel down the Tigris
or the Euphrates, to get to the Shatt al-Arab,
then, perhaps...do some floating...to reach Iran –
maybe jump onto one of the minesweepers...

His nose & forehead wrinkle.
She would have to get to a river with water, first.

Clifta is starting to spring about restlessly
on Max Strang's long black oily neck hairs
just above his open collar. Max is now talking to Weasel Smith's girlfriend, calling her
darling, very softly, over & over.
He does not seem to notice Clifta.
I've seen boats with thatched tops –
Iraqis living on them –
on one of the rivers,
Peter begins slowly. He is thinking
such a thatched top
would make a good place
for a spider to hide in,
Clifta stares at Peter. His eyes are big & dark.

He does not look like a Huntsman Spider.
He does not look at all like a great huntsman...
She begins to recite:
... They say the Lion and the Lizard
keep
The Courts where Jamshýd gloried
and drank deep:
And Bahrám, that great Huntsman –
the Wild Ass
Stamps o'er his Head, and he lies fast
asleep.
Peter looks hard at Clifta. He can see her better
now Max Strang has turned his neck.
The light from Max Strang's torch
makes scarlet specks glitter on her cargo pants
as she moves around his hair.
She will have to take those cargo pants off, Peter thinks,
if she is to travel
less noticeably
on the pale
desert sand. He asks
Are 'Jamshýd' & 'Bahrám' philosophers?

&, with less interest, belatedly,
because, after some thought,
he still does not understand:
What does your poem...mean?

Clifta does not answer directly.
She heard it from her mother,
while roaming in a Sydney park
around her mother's hairy legs
amid hundreds of other week-old sibling spiders.
She thinks she might be related
to the great Huntsman of the *Rubáiyát*. Since the poem
has been translated from the Persian, she has stowed away,
on the person of the newsman, & in his camera case,
to go to Persia, to try to gather 'facts'
for the Huntsman's Family Tree.

Journeys West of 'War'
2 What is 'The World'?

What is 'The World'?
Peter has read
in the Hindu Upanishads
that 'the world before creation
was water'. If you could find
'the world before creation', you could find
where water might have been
perhaps, & perhaps,
there might still be some there, he thinks.

He has been reading about the pre-
Socratic philosophers – east & west –
from some small books he found in English
in an empty house outside Baghdad,

& wondering, for the umpteenth time,
where his *Rabbit History of Philosophers*
should begin. Perhaps there was a primordial,
even famous, rabbit philosopher
from whom the Pre-Socratics
made their start?
When he talks of this to Clifta, she jumps sideways
& begins excitedly to talk.
She has an in-the-beginning story to tell.
Once was a female Huntsman Spider, from whose egg-sac

sprang earth, water, sky, & 'world', & from whom
the first lemon-scented gum trees grew, as well
as the angophoras, the acacias,
& the Sydney bluegums that were made
for Huntsman Spiders to live & hunt beneath.

Peter is reminded Clifta travelled to Iraq
under or around the collar of,
or perhaps, in the camera case that hung from,
Max Strang's hairy Sydney neck.
She is not an English spider.

He worries. If she is too small
to make a web, what does she eat?

They are travelling down the riverbed, looking
for the camel, in case it can be persuaded
to take Clifta, not to Baghdad, but to somewhere
lower down, where, on Peter's map, the Euphrates
has water, & there may be boats...
It's a city camel. Peter thinks it may not
have realised, initially, the north-western channels
have no water. Eventually, it, too, will need
to drink, it may, even now,
be travelling south & east...
Clifta is scuttling along, quite fast
but she never goes in a straight line
down the riverbed, she inspects behind rocks

& large pebbles. Each time, he
has to stop, & wait for her to re-emerge.
He has no idea what she is looking for.

They've left Max Strang, waiting for the desert hyenas
which he is hoping
to tape. They have seen no hyenas.
Max Strang was on his mobile again,
speaking softly to Weasel Smith's girlfriend,
trying to persuade her to give up on Weasel Smith
& come & join him, soon, in Iraq.
Peter's learnt Max has a ride
back to Baghdad, arranged with an Iraqi
who has camels, but who will not arrive
for about a week.
Max Strang is a patient man. He has
water & a tin pyramid of cans.
For hyenas he is
prepared to wait.
Clifta
had been impatient.
She'd wanted
to get off his neck.

It is not happy travelling. The sun moves slowly overhead.
Clifta's begun another recitation of the poem
Arachnid Fitzgerald translated from the Persian
& although there have been intermissions, when she scuttled,

Peter, by now, is becoming pretty bored with it.
He is also itchy, gritty, & more than a little hungry.
A wind has arisen, on the desert above,
which blows more sand into his fur, even though
they are below the worst of it. Faintly he hears
English voices, above the wind,
& struggles
through slipping sand
up the bank. The last two stragglers from the hiking group
of phenomenalist philosophers
have caught the reluctant camel. One is attempting
to drag it by a rope, dodging
its snorts & attempts to bite.
The other, doing nothing, stands well behind.
They are headed back towards Baghdad. Their water cans &
backpacks have been secured to the camel's sides.
Peter can hear the camel harrumphing crossly:
they have not thought to give it any water. Baghdad
is exactly where it does not want to go.
Abruptly it sits down, refusing to move.
What kind of 'Phenomenology'
are they studying? Peter wonders. He has read –
a very little – about Husserl's
'Realist Phenomenology', & that
Husserl maintained 'the mind'
& nothing else in 'the world'
has 'a directedness' towards something
outside itself. He thinks about the camel

which seems to be directed, now,
towards gaining water, & of Clifta
who seems to be directed backwards in time
towards locating an ancient starting point
of Huntsman Spiders...

Peter has no idea how many books
it might take to do
the Huntsman's Family Tree,
nor to trace Clifta's ancestors back
to the civilization
of Ancient Persia.
He has seen spiders' webs glistening at night
the lines going out...perhaps...towards
the stars; he imagines, though her search
could not be infinite, it might seem so...
Husserl wrote: there always has to be a
consciousness
        of something, & whether,
or not, there is a 'world of objects'
outside the objects of our consciousness,
can, quite simply, be bracketed out.

Clifta, Peter thinks, wants to find
something in 'the world
that is bracketed out'.
        If she
finds 'Persia',

she can, perhaps,
gain sense-data
about her ancestor,
the Huntsman of the *Rubáiyát*,
& she won't need to prove,
Peter thinks, with effort,
that her 'facts'
'exist'
outside her consciousness...

From the channel of the Euphrates, he sees
her tiny indignant form emerge. *I want to go to Persia NOW,*
she says. The English philosophers
have given up,
have unloaded the camel, & abandoned it. They
have taken their desert-sand-coloured selves
in their pale sandals
away, quite fast. The camel staggers up.
There is water in the river
to the south-east, Peter says. *If you take me – &*, he points, to the
agitated tiny spider, *I think I can find*
the main channel of the Euphrates, where we can drink. If we
follow it down to the Delta, there'll be date palms, shelter
& plants to eat... He turns to face Clifta.
In the Delta, you will be closer to 'Persia' –
it is called 'Iran' now – &, in the Hawr al-Hammar,
there may be many boats...

The Camel

The camel has never been to the Shatt al-Arab.
It wants to ruminate on whether it wants to go.

Can you ride a camel? Peter Henry Lepus asks.
Clifta does not answer.

It turns out she doesn't want to,
though she will ride clinging to him

if he stays very still on its back,
& the camel walks **v e r y s l o w l y.**

She's fearful of falling off
& of being crushed.
The camel has not agreed
to take them beyond

the main channel
of the Euphrates.

It decides it does not want travel
to the Hawr al-Hammar,

which, it believes, is located
to the north & west

of the Shatt al-Arab –
though it is not sure.

... In addition, it has heard stories

from some of the Bazaar's camels...
about the water drying up...the Hawr al-Hammar

may not be there anymore.
About the Shatt al-Arab, too, it has doubts,

but it does not tell Peter
what these are. Now,

it is thirsty. It wants to find water.

When Peter & Clifta
unsuspectingly get off it, it leaves them at a trot.

Journeys West of 'War'
3 'South'?

Travel

Peter has been meditating
on the first line
of Wittgenstein's *Tractatus*...*The world*
is all that is the case.
                    In 'Logic'
everything that 'is'
contains the possibility
of 'isn't',
of being absent,
of not existing, Peter thinks.

His paws
are sore. He & Clifta
are heading
            towards where,
on an ancient map, the Euphrates'
                    dry channel
joins the watered one.
It is not
      the case
that the ground's
become less hard.

Each day,
his paws
feel the riverbed's
adamantine stones
grow hotter
as the day wears on.

Clifta has two of her eyes,
the biggest, focused on one track,
Peter sees, turning back, to look for her.
She's scuttling flat out, between the banks,
straight down centre-river.
Peter wonders,
with hope & some uncertainty,
is she sensing, now,
what he can't –
the far-off water's ways
to what is now Iran,
(&, once,
was Ancient Persia)
where he, perhaps,
may need to go,
to finish his entry
on Zarathustra?

As he hops,
he has been making suppositions about spiders,
some of whom have six, eight, ten or twelve eyes,

& puzzling, if Clifta grows more,
how she will use them;
what...will she see?

———

He & Clifta
have decided to travel
mostly in the cooler dark,
mainly because,
though Clifta's now reconciled
to riding clinging to his fur
(even while he is running,
hopping,
or bounding from rock
to rock)
its individual hairs,
as the sun heats up,
grow uncomfortably wet & slippery;
they do not shade her much.

He's become less concerned
about the colour of Clifta's cargo pants;
their scarlet glitter
helps him to see where she is
when she's exploring
the riverbed in the starlit after-dark.
He's seen no birds, migratory or of the desert,
either by day or night; un-reinforced,

his worries
that a curious
or hungry one
might swoop
on a conspicuously-
scarlet
tiny
Huntsman

have gone.

They stop a little before dawn.
Peter crouches behind a large rock,
worrying he & Clifta
might meet the hyenas
Max Strang hopes to tape. They fall asleep.

When Peter first wakes in the riverbed's early light,
he's been dreaming of Wittgenstein's face: the whites
of W.'s eyes were turned to one side, staring fixedly
towards something Peter could not see.
W. was wearing a jacket of knobbly wool
that Russell said was 'tweed'; the colours
so unlike the cloudless blue
of the desert sky,
or the mistless green
of Baghdad trees, remind Peter
of other skies, & softer English hillsides.
Any grass would be welcome now, he thinks,

drifting into dreamless sleep.

When next his eyes open,
Clifta's sprung onto his left front paw,
& is trying to tap him awake – quickly – with one of her legs.
She's very excited. She wants him to look at
something she's found.

Hidden
by the tall boulder
she leads him to,
wedged, between it
& the riverbed's
sheltering wall,
Peter sees a large blue-plastic backpack.
It is broken-strapped,
heavy,
& heat-cracked. Maps fatten
its open side-flap pockets.
Book spines poke through its splits.
With many kicks,
he manages to manoeuvre it sideways.
Clifta springs back
as the pockets' multi-folded maps tumble out.
Many of them are thick,
taller than she is. They are *not*
what she wants him to look at. Beside the pack,
she's found, on a sheet of white paper,

a huge picture of a Huntsman Spider,
but
the writing
is in a language
she cannot read.
She wants to know: *is it*
her ancestor, *the Huntsman*
of the Rubáiyát?
Peter has watched the hand
of an Arab scholar
making curving script
from right to left
across a page more difficult
than anything
Peter thinks he'll ever
learn   to understand...*That* writing
looked like the writing under Clifta's picture.
I have not learnt to read Arabic, he says.

Backpack

Clifta crawls slowly & dejectedly
        to squat
on top of the picture. Peter begins to search
for what else
the pack might hold. He finds a bag
labelled 'breakfast oats', a corked,

half-litre
of 'Stilled Springs Water', & a tin
labelled 'milk'.
He can use the oats & the water.

Digging further, he discovers
dried fruit, an empty dish,
stapled sheets of writing,
in clear plastic wraps,
& many fat folders.

One, which is black-tied,
he struggles to undo;
outside on the sand-coloured cardboard
is written:
Mesopotamian Marshlands
of the Tigris-Euphrates Delta;
inside
are picture maps
dated March, two thousand & three.

There are names & addresses
        of *scientists*
on some of its documents.

A few of these names
he finds again,
                on reports

about something called 'biome'.

Articles
downloaded from the internet,
headed 'Saddam Hussein's'

or sometimes
'The Iraqi Government's'

WATER CONTROL PROJECTS,

are interspersed
with hand-written pages
in purple ink
that's blurred,
or pooled in lakes, then dried
with many words inbetween crossed out...*Saddam...*
mustard...the blistered face of the Kurdish child ...
then, after words – scratched out
so vehemently that the paper's holed – *the health*
of the entire Iraqi people...chemistry...
suspected poured into rivers...disposed of underground.
The next three pages are stuck together.

Peter Henry cannot read them
so he puts them down.

Glancing at the start
of an extract from a long report:
The Third World Water Forum,
Kyoto, Japan,
he notices, after recurrent reference
to the 'Tigris-Euphrates Delta Marshland',
an unfamiliar word, '**desertification**',
then another, '**salination**', but
without the dictionary he left in Baghdad
he cannot look them up.

Next, there are two pink maps
from the Iraqi Foundation,
with *Albu Ayish, September 1998,*
& Albu Ayish, December 1999,
printed beneath. On the second of these,
black arrows point
to yellow-green
burrow-like mounds
where humans' houses
have been squashed.

Peter wonders, since it does not say,
if the humans were inside when the squashings happened,
& thinks, that, if they were,
perhaps they, too, were squashed.
It is where the Ma'dan live.

It is not a part of the Marshlands
he has visited. He remembers,
in nineteen eighty-nine,
Ma'dan houses –
        different kinds –
each with a fence of goldbrown reeds;
                                        going down
                                        straight into water,
& sometimes on these fences he'd seen
the Marshlands' sacred ibis perch
& groom their drying feathers.
        Where he was – then –
the Ma'dan used slim boats & poles
to get from house to house.
        He'd ridden in one of their boats – once –
hiding in a gold reed basket,
propelled, with a load of finished mats,
by Ma'dan men,
        along waterways
that smelled like wet-feathered ibis;
lulled by the sounds of Arabic
he'd slept, not knowing where
they were going.
        He'd stayed with them
when they'd left the boat – undetected –
bound for a Fertile Crescent market.

The squashed houses,

on the second pink map, have yellow grass around them
that a camel could walk on, carrying Clifta...maybe
as far as the Hawr al-Hammar...

There are no Ma'dan to be seen.
Which part of the Delta are they in, he wonders.
Perhaps it is in the study inscribed MA'DAN...

There is nothing
on *this* folder's map, or, in the caption under it,
that would tell him
if the yellow grassland stretches as far as the Hawr al-Hammar

but there are studies headed ECOLOGY,
ENVIRONMENT,
& pages & pages
of **Information on Spiders**.

A Digression...?

He will have to be careful telling Clifta
about what's in the pack, he thinks. Clifta
wants to avoid 'scientists'
& 'science laboratories', while in Iraq.
Peter remembers why.

While she was on the plane from Australia & peering

out, through Max Strang's hair, over his shoulder
at a person
in the seat behind, she saw
                                        that person examining
a photo
of a grown-up Heteropoda Huntsman Spider,
its legs pushed up against the too-narrow walls
of a glass tube,
                                        in which
it was unable to move,
                              & around which curled
the long pink fingers of a scientist
who was holding the tube upright
on a work bench
in a laboratory:
                    she realised
that the person looking *at* the photo
was the same as the one *in* the photo, a scientist,

& perhaps the Huntsman had been trapped by him, ***to die***.

Even having overheard lengthy
& complex discussions
of spider morphology,
by passengers with baggage labelled
'**Dr**'...
'**Arachnid Conference**, **Qatar**',
on the plane in which

he'd travelled to Turkey,
Peter Henry knows little
of scientists who trap spiders;
he hopes Clifta
                will not meet
many more of them on her journey.

Referring to...

The creamy oats are good, & very fresh.
He eats almost all of them,
& manages to tug the bottle's cork out,
spilling some water
into the dish, so he can drink.

Then he begins to study
the fat folder's many maps.

It takes him a long time to read them.
English-lettered 'Arabic' names,
al-Basrah, Hawr al-Hawizeh, Hawr al-Azim,
differ from the ones
in the books from London
he's read in the empty house outside Baghdad.
Still, he thinks,
they must name the same ground...or water...
He reads on,

becoming less certain...

& then there are the ones
named 'satellite image',
also dated March, two thousand & three,
some in browns & blues & greens,
others in shades
like sunsets he's seen,
which the maps in small letters
in corners
call 'false colours'.

On these,
there are no rivers,
lakes,
or places named.

He cannot find the Hawr al-Hammar.

How can he tell Clifta, he wonders,
looking towards
where he last saw her,

perhaps the Hawr al-Hammar
does not
        exist any more...

He remembers the camel's tales

of water

disappearing

from the Delta.

He knows the camel
had not seen this for itself.

Then, he'd thought its stories
might have been,
because, being thirsty,
it'd wanted to get back
to the riverways it knew.
Its home, he remembers,
was a city in the lands between
the *watered* Euphrates & the Tigris,
not far below Baghdad.

But perhaps, he puzzles to himself,
the Hawr al-Hammar

is like Russell's 'The present king of France is wise'

when there is *no* 'present king of France' – a structure
existing only in language, referring to NOTHING

& to have read

the Hawr al-Hammar

as a '*representation of reality*'

was, therefore, **wrong**?

He remembers telling Clifta:
In the Hawr al-Hammar, there may be

many boats...thinking, there, she'd find one
to Iran...*How*
will she get there now?

Where is she? No longer brooding on top of
the picture of her ancestor, Peter sees; the portrait
is now unadorned
by Clifta's tiny red-cased legs. He catches a glimpse
of the red spot of her cargo pants
disappearing
round the back of a rock. He is starting to follow her
when he hears a camel snort,
& then another.
Max Strang, under a battered Akubra,
& mounted on a trotting camel,
is coming round the nearest bend.
quite fast. There's an Iraqi with him,
& further back, a camel that carries a load
but has no rider.

Max

Max Strang
has given up
on trying to tape
the Western Desert's hyenas.
Thinks
they might be extinct
in the area
where he made his camp.
He's talkative,
since he's been picked up.
As they ride, he learns,
from Hamid
who owns the camels, hyenas
used to roam
the deserts
to the south   between the freshwater lakes
& the saltmarshes
of the Tigris-Euphrates Wetlands...*before they were drained,*
by constructions & diversions,
Hamid said, *to 'punish' the Ma'dan*
who'd risen against Saddam
during the Gulf War, in anticipation of
a Saddam-free Iraq.

Many of his walls & dams
've now been smashed, Hamid adds. *The water's trickling back*

from the snow melt in the Zagors & Anatolian mountains.
Some places, there's a flow...
Where water was, where it is now
is changing, the UN map-makers can't keep up with it.
May be a few hyenas left down there, the Iraqi says,
may be some money in it for you,
worth, perhaps – the risks involved
in trying
to travel south.

He & Max've spent the previous night
as guests of a sheikh
(of Hamid's tribe but not his clan);
they have bathed, & feasted
on freshly killed sheep;
slept comfortable, & clean, & before noon
witnessed meetings,
as the sheikh's clansmen
brought their concerns,
(from familial proposals to truck-thefts)
for adjudication
to the sheikh's *mudhef.*

Hamid translated for Max:
much of what was said
was about getting supplies by road
to & from Basrah.

Max says: *By air is out*. He's heard
the Baghdad airport's
under frequent rocket attack,
commercially unsafe
& closed, still, *except*
'to war-related flights', though *Basrah's*
operational, &,
as well as connecting with Braid,
he *wouldn't mind*
                    getting one or two
discordant,
                    southern wetlands' waterbirds
on tape,
particularly those
                    threatened with extinction,
                    maybe record the calls
of the Garden of Eden's last sacred ibis...
His *muso friend at Griffith*
might be in the market, too,   *for that.*

But, Max tells Hamid firmly
my prime aim   *is locating Braid*.

Using the Baghdad-bought
mobile with aerial,
its box clumsily balanced
on his saddle's pommel,
Max's been back (almost compulsively) in touch

with an English journalist friend, he's learnt
is now reporting on
'security problems'
                        besetting
                                the British based in Basrah:
'the lack of law': the need to establish
safer streets, the setting up
of patrols in pairs – :
one British one Iraqi –

the perhaps unstoppable
sabotage
of the oil pipelines – ...who knows by whom?

Max's heard, independently, that security guards
've been hired, from outside Iraq, & 're coming in
to patrol pipelines north of Basrah. He thinks
Braid might've talked her way
into coming in, with them.
She's got a way with words.
He's emailed Weasel Smith in Sydney,
from the sheikh's, to try to find out where she is,
without actually asking.
(Weasel's last mobile conversations to him in the desert
'd been about what a good fuck Braid was – to compensate
for her absence from his bed, he'd taken to going out at night
& shooting possums).

'Wease' had emailed back:
Braid's got a promise of work as a stringer;
she wants to do 'an environmental piece'
on 'The World Ecological Disaster' – the 'former Wetlands'...
Braid's told Max she's
had it with Weasel & whether
                    or not
                              it works out,
                                        between her & Max,
she is never going back to Weasel. She wants to break the
        news to him from a distance
because of his bad temper.
Thinking of how close she may be, Max begins to goad his
        camel to go faster.
I need to get to Baghdad soon,
he tells the Iraqi, *I've got a meeting with a Yank*
I met in one of the markets,
after that...I'm heading south.
but when he talks to Weasel Smith
he does not mention this;
he talks, instead, of leads for feature stories,
which he's already started files for,
on a battery-powered notebook,
while waiting for hyenas
in the days when he was camped.

West of Al Shualla

Are all Arabs Muslims? Peter Henry asks.
Nobody answers him.
She's got dark hair that stops
just above her shoulders. Turns up at the ends.
She's very slim, Max says.
He's talking to Hamid
about Weasel Smith's girlfriend,
whom he is hoping to meet
somewhere south of Baghdad.

Do you have a wife in Australia? Hamid
politely asks.
Max snorts, Peter thinks, like one
of Hamid's camels. Then, less rudely,
I'm not married, Max says, *though I might*
if it works out with Braid.
Looking from one
to the other, they are sitting on same-size camels,
Peter sees Hamid
looks much bigger
        & taller
                than Max;
                        he remembers
his mother's puzzled recall
of an oral lore,
        passed down

from unknowable rabbits,
living
perhaps centuries
before:

It is not polite
to be rude to those
who are
larger
than oneself.

He remembers, too, that,
though she kicked with extreme ferocity,
when tunnelling earth,
& could, in adversarial conversations,
be vigorous, as well as firm,
she'd not been rude to anyone.

Peter has been studying his notebook,
somewhat awkwardly, from the back
of the third camel. Clifta – minus her cargo pants –
is hiding under the pommel. He has noticed,
since she's grown a little taller,
they have not fitted her well.

There is a dead Iraqi
wrapped in Max's plastic ground sheet
roped stiffly to the camel's side.

Return to Baghdad
I Regressive – Near the Euphrates – Finding the Dead Iraqi

They found him
several hundred metres on
from where Max'd dismounted.
I need, he'd said, *to stretch my legs*.
The riverbed there was sand.
They were quite close to the Euphrates.
Peter could smell its water.
Hamid called out, surprised
into Arabic, which Peter knew
was not
how Hamid
usually talked to Max.
He'd listened to them
earlier in the day
discussing the backpack's contents at length,
including some I.D. cards
in a pouch he'd overlooked. All of which
Max'd eventually lifted easily,
only needing to use one arm,
swinging it up,
heavy as Peter thought it was, casually
onto the third camel's back.
Hamid had spent some time securing it.
It may be

of some value
to its owner, Hamid had said...

though...to return it
could prove risky;

whatever name he uses...
if he was here last year,
he's likely to be followed...

perhaps even
by someone vengeful
from the former secret police.

Ready to leave, already ensconced on the third camel,
Clifta had shown increasing distress,
racing to & fro across the baggage,
whether in rage or grief, Peter'd not, initially,
been able to tell.
Eventually he saw.
It had been some distance from the pack.
Max had not noticed it.
Turned face-side up to the fierce blue desert sky,
Clifta's photo of her 'ancestor',
the great
'Huntsman of the *Rubáiyát*',
had been left behind.

There was sand in his eyes
when Hamid turned him.
Black blood had gone into the ground.
He'd a bullet hole in his back.
He's been tortured, Hamid said.

There were flies, Peter saw,
but he did not know, then
that the flies were coming to death.

2 Closer to the Tigris

A miserable dog howls to the west
somewhere behind them,
as they skirt the city's northern fringes, warily
looking for a dark way in
to Joshua Smith's.
Clifta & Peter lurk on the back of the third camel,
roped, with a long lead,
to the one Max rides.
Max & Hamid's camels travel abreast.
They are moving quite fast,
& Clifta's jumping about,
close to Peter's nose, on a tilting sat-dish
as if she would like to spring off.
The air smells disturbingly of smoke, garbage,
& something which Peter does not recognise,
which seems to come directly
from the groundsheet's wrapping at their camel's side.
Max & Hamid turn back frequently
to eye the third camel's progress.
Peter can hear them muttering
& taking deep sniffs of the air.
Several times Max leans to one side of his camel
rasping...as if he's trying to be sick...
but he & Hamid do not stop.

The standing houses they trot by have dark windows.

In some places, lines of four or five joint-walled houses
have vanished into bomb-cratered ground.
The camels' pace must slacken:
there are also pit-like holes in the road,
which the first two camels step cautiously round.
Peter thinks, if his & Clifta's camel
fell
into one of these holes,
it probably...wouldn't get out...
Occasionally the eastern sky is lit by rockets
& there are closer muffled explosions
that bring no light.

Some yards have broken walls,
which their unworried camel steps over,
but the ground inside is always hard or paved
& yields no grass to its searching mouth.

Peter catches a rare glimpse,
in a kerosene-lamp-lit doorway's yellowy glow,
of the long dark curling hairs
at the back of Max Strang's hatless head; he is glad
Max has lost his Akubra. Perhaps
he put it down
when the three camels had their drink...Peter
is not fond of Akubras. He recalls some unpleasant lines
from an Australian poet he has read...which begin, to him
incomprehensibly:
Half Acrostic/ Peter's Rue

Actually
Knife
Un-
Body
Rabbit
Alas

Peter's Rue:

it takes
fifteen rabbits
skint
of
THEIR LIVES
to make
one
never-alive
Akubra
hat

He hopes, from the deep coils of his innards,
that Max never finds
another Akubra hat.

They'd had a fire & Max'd done some cooking
the day the Euphrates was reached. Water was boiled
& water bottles refilled...for the journey east to the Tigris.
Peter thinks mournfully of the last three powdery mouth-fulls

of the backpack's breakfast oats,
which he's long ago finished,
& less mournfully,
though not with much hope,
that they are now deep into Baghdad,
& may find food
in Joshua Smith's onion-domed burrow-like house.

Mio Palazzo

Mio palazzo, says the Abyssinian,
peering out,
        way above,
                from a
                      l
                      o
                      n
                      g
                      dark
                      rectilinear frame.

She's sunk, bottom-left,
in a huge wooden doorway,
but only the top-third's lit.

Peter can see, very clearly, she is CAT,
though a strange one.

Is she talking...to him?

Above where he squats –
& deeper inside the building
than he's
yet explored –
semi-smashed

oat-cream steps
            lead
                        to an upper floor.
A skinny long-tailed rat
                        hurtles up them,
its skittering sending out grit, some stones,
& dust in random oat-cream clouds.

Bits of stone fall sideways
as Peter hops, cautiously curious,
after the rat. He'd wondered
how Joshua got to the top,
to open the dome's
small pale-green 'onion' windows
that let in the bats
& the winds that cooled.

In the ground-floor kitchen,
where he'd left Clifta running in
& out of one of the cupboards,
there'd been a lot of breeze.

A second long-tailed rat
leaps up the broken stairs, bolting
over the paws of the unmoving cat.
                        I do not eat
rat, mouse, pig, cat – or rabbit –
she says with an imperial whiskerly twitch,

apparently directed towards Peter,
a little as if he might be...the visitor...
perhaps, even a supplicant...
who is, unknowingly, bringing
inapposite gifts.
Have you any fish? Fish
will do.
But Peter does not answer her.

Mio palazzo, she says again,
inclining her head towards him,
to indicate, with a swish of her tail,
the direction in which the second rat
has run. She's standing very tall,
to one side of the doorway, so she's facing Peter
from the left. It seems she wants him to come in.
He watches her eyes,
& seeing she's not in a hunting crouch,
edges past, keeping well to the right
of her claws, as he enters, for the first time,
what lies beneath
the high-up 'onion' windows. Except for some
closed wooden crates   with **DATES** printed on them,
FOR EXPORT stencilled smaller, & a few boxes –
with books strewn around or stacked
in crooked piles coming out of the boxes' open tops –
towards which both rats have run,
& where it seems they've been dragging chewed-off pages

for a nest – there's no furniture
in all that upper floor's long darkish space.

Beneath it lie the bedrooms
of Joshua's fifteen wives.

In one far part of it, Peter sees,
where the building's side's been torn away,
the roof has fallen down.

It does not look at all
like the only other palace Peter's seen

which was in photos Max Strang had,
that he said he'd *'borrowed' from US marines,*

& which, Max'd said, was a
reconstruction,

of Nebuchadnezzar's
ancient Babylonian palace –

built, in 'modern' Babylon
under order by,
& for
Saddam Hussein.
There was a room inside it –
vast, like this one – but differenced by a golden thing

that Max had called a 'throne',   wide, he'd said,
                              as the front
                              of an old-time
                              Sydney slum –
but all the inner walls were gold.

No one lived there.
Saddam had many palaces, Max said.
                              Now, he's on the run.

Peter remembers earlier he's heard
Max on his sat-phone, to Weasel Smith in Sydney,
telling him that the 'new' palace
meant to last a thousand years
was built of bricks so shonky
the lower outer walls had cracked
after only ten;
        behind & between
the broken bricks, there might be places
someone might hide
some stolen Mormon plates...
hiding gold   under   painted gold...Could be
a suitable site for him & Joshua Smith to search.
Might be a feature story there, happier
than certain others he could write...
Controversial too, or could be made to seem so...
Was the original (safely dead)

Founder of the Mormons **(*Joseph* Smith)**
Lunatic? Con man? Or martyred (murdered)
Quasi-Saint? A bit crass, but someone might buy it.

Weasel hadn't seemed to disagree: if a story
turned up good enough, he'd a friend
'on the inside', he claimed, 'at the *PseudWeekend*';
if Max sent the feature story to Weasel,
rather than direct, he'd 'broker the deal'.

Peter remembers, almost word for word,
what Max had said, & Weasel – louder –
he'd been close to them, in a room below
where he & the cat are now,
finishing the wilted top of a carrot,
Josh having left at dawn to get more food,
Hamid & the still-hungry camels
being camped at the back of the Baghdad house...
Max at work on his 'feature story', listening
to Josh's voice on tape telling of his search
for his missing wives
& their search
for the sacred Mormon text
(inscribed on the two gold plates)
which might, perhaps,
'justify' plural marriage.

The Abyssinian is patiently watching Peter.

She seems to want him to talk.
At last he manages: *Have you always*
lived up here? Alone?

She lowers herself from her tall & stately pose
to a comfortable crouch.
Explains. She does not 'belong' to the man below.
She has simply 'taken up residence' above him.

Formerly she lived
with an Iraqi scientist, who was developing masks
for the Iraqi army to wear.
The successful masks
would be taken away.
Only a higher ranked scientist
who'd made a whispered phone call
knew
when & where
the masks
would go.
The scientist whose room she shared would turn & watch
behind him when he walked outside by day or night.
His hands shook when he gave her food.
He no longer talked
to friends by phone. Then the *Mukhabarat*
came to find him, but he wasn't there. She
didn't see him again. She's heard he's now
a prisoner on Nauru.

Peter, who knows nothing of Nauru, has nothing to contribute.
He finds the severity of the Abyssinian's stare,
the fact that her gaze never leaves his face, unnerving.
Though her stillness works to allay his fears about her,
he has been listening to her uneasily,
not knowing if there's a hungry, second cat that's been out
        scouting
& is about to bound back silently, springing at him
through the gloomy doorway.
It's very quiet, except for the soft sound
of the Abyssinian's head,
which may be itchy since she's rubbing it
against the nearest wall.
                                        Peter,
though he hopes to keep his experience of cats
to a minimum, is emboldened
to persist: *Do you live up here **alone**?*
Yes. She is a spinster aunt, she says,
with two sisters, & many nieces & nephews,
who used to visit her, only one
of whom
she's seen, since the 'war', which she's heard
but not really 'viewed'. *I was asleep*
& did not wake up
for over a day
when part of the building fell in. I woke
down below with an ache in my head...
It is better now.

She turns her head to show Peter
the wound, some skin, semi-bare,
with short hairs growing back.
I am a red or sorrel Abyssinian, she says.
We came from Egypt long ago, my maternal line
centred somewhere round Alexandria...
though much time has passed;
there's a story her mother told, long handed down,
that one of their matrilineal line
was a follower of a philosopher
who belonged to a secret sect
& went out
with him
into the desert
to where the sect met
though she did not understand
what they said. She lived
with the philosopher's daughter, Hypatia,
a mathematician who wrote commentaries
on the geometries
of Apollonius & Diophantus
about whom, in the Alexandrian
'world' of the Sorrel Abyssinians,
not much was known & little said.

Why I have no children, I do not know.

Peter does not know why either.

Carefully, one ear drooping down as he considers
what he does not understand, he asks:
Would having children bring you food?
What...do you eat?
She purrs, dismissively, *one...of his wives...*
used to bring me food...

Peter has spied a heavy,
partly kernel-chewed-out
corncob segment
one of the rats must've dropped,
but does not like to venture...so far...
into '*Mio Palazzo*' (away
from the door)
to taste-test it,
in case the Abyssinian's purring stops.

He thinks she is wrong about Hypatia
(whom he has been considering
for inclusion
in his *History of Philosophers* –
as well, perhaps, as Plato –)
since his readings have led him to believe
Hypatia was a philosopher,
a Neo-Plato-nist, who taught
at the Philosophy School in
Alexandria, but that all her works,
except the one on mathematics & the conic section,

were destroyed, when the Library
at Alexandria burned.

Peter Henry tries again with the cat
who is still purring very slightly, though her face
seems to him to have become sad. *Does Joshua come up here
to bring you food?* he asks.
Abruptly the mood changes.
Unpredictably the Abyssinian's tail begins to lash the floor.
    Her body stiffens. Her gaze,
though it is directed through the doorway, & not at Peter,
    worries him,
since it assumes a rather fierce expression
of displeasure – or disdain. Perhaps
it is directed towards the absent Joshua?

I am reduced, at last she responds, *to relying*
                                        exclusively
on a diet of Baghdad lizards, for which
I have to descend
these dangerously-stone-powdered stairs. My red sorrel fur

is always dirty, because of them, & however hard I bite a Baghdad lizard,
it never smells of the Atlantic

like those tiny cans of lobster & crab
that man's fifteenth wife
used to smuggle up to me. She was pregnant...

The stairs were hard for her. They were not broken, then...

I wish

that she would remember me...& return
to Mio Palazzo.
Because she does not come,
I am afraid...she may be dead...

Thales of the Pre-Socratics

I

Thales was an early rabbit, who told
that EVERYTHING, when you chewed, squashed,
or pounded it,
        broke down
                to water.

Peter has already drafted this entry
(& a few others)
                tentatively

for his *History of Philosophers*,

before he discovers
                there is no mention
in any of the extant texts,
                by 'early philosophers',
who were later
than Thales,
                that Thales was a rabbit.

It seems, he writes, no texts by Thales survive.
Then pauses, re-reading some
of his later entries...

regressing to Thales...

who may

have been born at 'Miletus',

a place in 'Asia Minor',

in B.C. six hundred

& twenty-five,

& who also was famous – Peter's nose

tilts gravely down as he inspects his notes –

for predicting

what Russell explained

was the 'first'

(known to Western humans by date)

'solar eclipse' –

in B.C. five hundred & eighty-five –

It seems the fierce Medes & Lydians

were having a sunlit fight

&, when the sun went dark,

they stopped & went home

perhaps because they couldn't see

to kick & bite.

This happened when Thales said it would,

& has been recorded, Peter's notes reveal,

by Nicholas Fearn*,

* Nicholas Fearn is the author of *zeno and the tortoise* (Atlantic Books, Great Britain, 2001). Peter has not read *zeno and the tortoise*, but his English research assistant, Picasso Rabbit, has advised him that it contains reference to Thales. Picasso has kindly included, with this information, notes about Thales from a wide range of sources, most of which Peter has read but decided not to use.

as well as in what Herodotus wrote, on page seventy of
The Histories, published by Penguin (Classics)
in nineteen seventy-two (revised).

2

Peter's been pondering the story
that Thales fell into a big hole,
                              like ones
that people
in some countries
Peter's visited recently
had drawn their water from & called a well.

He thinks
                              that
if
              Thales
                              fell

a long way down –
                              & then   found water –
up to his neck –
perhaps this   was what made him think
that water...was under everything.
But this was something Thales **believed**.
He had not chewed, squashed, or pounded
      E V E R Y T H I N G.

There are too many of them, too many THINGS,
Peter Henry decides,
        & – especially – Thales
was wrong about sand – in the season without rain
in the Iraqi Western desert:

                if sand is chewed,
                        squashed,
                                or pounded,

no water will come from it. He has tried.

Two Days After They Arrive in Baghdad

Max & Hamid have returned
to the morgue, this time with the camel.
Peter, staying discreetly further back
crouched behind a parked Citroën,
& peering through the gap
made by Max's slightly bandy legs,
in unwashed 'desert' jeans,
has watched them unrope the re-wrapped body
& lower it gently to the ground. It's shortly after dawn, & cooler.
Dark splashes of something came from inside the groundsheet.
Hamid keeps the camel still
but did not tell it to sit. Then
he goes into the morgue, while Max stands by the body
shifting his weight from foot to foot, gazing about.
People are coming in & out. Many are weeping.

A coffin, Max mutters, half turning. Peter, looking
in the direction Max is, sees an ancient rusted
green Toyota with a long wooden box roped to its roof.
Young Iraqi men in jeans are making it firmer with extra rope.
Where did they get the coffin? Max wonders aloud.
He is still holding the camel's lead but absently. Peter notices
    the camel
's moving slightly closer to the morgue, there are some shrubs,
    perhaps edible,

nearby, but also people lying unmoving on the ground.
He thinks it is trying to lead Max away from the ground-
sheeted body. Just then,
Hamid comes out. Max hands him
the camel's lead & strides curiously in,
through the morgue's open side door. Peter changes position,
moving
nearer – under the empty part where a load would go –
at the back of a battered truck parked close, right by
the morgue.
Severe-faced men are placing tiny pieces of human babies on
metal trays
which they slide into a refrigerator. It looks as if
each blackened bit, or pale or bloody blob
has its own metal tray; on one, there's a tiny ear.
Max has said something in Arabic to one of the men.
When he sees the tray with the ear, Max's face twists oddly –
as if he's about to weep, or trying not to. Peter has seen
a similar expression, once, on a philosopher's face.
Max turns to leave,
abruptly, without
waiting for an answer.
Peter sees the man bend
& spit at Max.
The gobbet lands
on Max's shoe.

Dilemma?

They'd talked long
in the pre-dawn hours of the day before
of what
to do with the dead man. Who was he?
They did not know his clan, what place he came from
nor his proper name.
His family should be told, Hamid'd said,
so they & those who know him
can come to the mosque & watch him washed,
in the washing room; there are customs
to be observed. We have special rites & prayers.

Peter who'd been crunching green fallout
from a box of the Kurdish beans
Max'd brought, for the absent,
still night-street-searching Josh,
'd seen how Hamid's weary eyes blazed at Max. *You have not*
been to an Iraqi's funeral yet, my friend. You do not understand...

If those who did this wrong to him are not punished
on this earth, Allah will exact retribution

Max is sitting cross-legged on the floor, his shoulders drooping.
Peter thinks he is talking aloud to himself, as Josh sometimes did.
He does not seem to want to respond to Hamid, so perhaps
he wasn't listening. His words follow a different path:

Should the dead man go to the morgue before
he's carried to the mosque? Might someone perhaps
come looking for a missing man & claim him?

———

They did not know his clan, nor how to find
his proper name.

———

He should be cleansed with soap,
rubbed with oils & wrapped in white, Hamid said.
That part's do-able, Max decided,
over-riding Hamid's doubt, ignoring the strange
expression on his face.
When Max tried, in the walled yard at the back of Josh's,
to slide the body out or peel the groundsheet off it,
Hamid proved to be right.
Peter, who'd thought
Max was about to wash the body,
had seen they were both wearing
cloths tied round their faces, which covered their noses; & that
Max seemed reluctant to pick up the soap
Hamid had brought.

Peter'd not met the smell the dead man made before.
Soft, wet bits of him stuck to the groundsheet or oozed.
Decomposition's set in, Max conceded,
turning away. *He's too far gone to be washed.*

They'd floated him to get the blood from the wounds
when they reached the Euphrates.
The water'd stopped the flies. They'd had nothing
to wrap him in but the plastic groundsheet. He'd been
tied back into it, wet. *A mistake*,
Max conceded, sharing this error, too, with Hamid.

When Max exits the morgue the following day
with the spittle on his shoe, he collects the
camel's lead from Hamid's hand, tugs its head away
from the bushes it is grazing by the door, which Peter sees
annoys it, & leads it out on to the road, following the route
back to Josh's house. Hamid follows, slightly further behind
& Peter scuttles after him, following the shade, from
    underneath one
to another parked car.
Peter wonders if they will return for the ground-sheeted body,
when it is cooler but they do not.

Archival

In Joshua's
large,
currently food-bare,
wife-deserted kitchen,
        Peter
has been reading notes
about Ya´qūb ibn Ishāq al-Kindī,
'the philosopher of the Arabs', who died
in the third century
of the Muslim calendar,
& who's one of three
        distinguished
                Islamic philosophers
        Peter wants to research
                at the University of Baghdad.

In his night explorations,
he's discovered
that the University out-buildings, where he'd hoped to work,
have had their insides burnt...perhaps by 'war' ?...
        & overheard, nearby, one journalist tell another
            sotto voce at an egg-&-bread-roll stall:
                The missile strike occurred
during the Assault on Baghdad. Seems
some known
semi-government personnel

had been seen

by Coalition informants, a.k.a. spies,

transferring boxes

by the truckload

from their office

to the out-buildings...

Contents: unknown.

Projection: records.

Further projection:

the boxes were either necessary

to the Government's functioning – therefore

crucial to keep safe – or,

(if the 'Invasion of Iraq', following 'Shock & Awe' succeeded)

they contained what the Government sought to hide –

Peter's been doing his own moving of records,
making careful journeys after dark,
scary late-night street trips
back to the empty house where he found the books in English
which he's brought back one by one to Josh's kitchen,
storing them
in a cupboard where some tiny wraith-like insects used to live,
white-wrapped on a crisp brown leaf
that he'd once seen Clifta resting quietly near.
There is little on al-Kindī in the books he's found.
He remembers Russell saying – he has noted it –
that al-Kindī, who 'translated parts
of the *Enneads* of Plotinus'

from Greek

into Arabic,

'published his translation under the title: *The Theology of Aristotle*'.

Why? Peter asks himself. Then,
reading more he's noted from Russell,
he thinks he understands: Plotinus,
who worked on parts
of the writings by Aristotle, drew the lines of
of its thinking forward, developing
or disagreeing with the arguments Aristotle wrote,
which were about many things,
including writing by Plato.

The learned al-Kindī
did not have Aristotle's writings in Greek or in Arabic
& drew his 'knowing' of Aristotle's philosophy
only from Plotinus...perhaps?

But, Peter hesitates, diffident, thinking carefully, Russell wrote
that the Syrians –
before the Muslim conquest – favoured the work of Aristotle
in preference to the work of Plato, **both of whom wrote in Greek**,
so perhaps...there was an early Syrian scholar
who knew both Greek & the ancient language of Syria
& had translated *some*
of Aristotle's work as well as *some* of Plato's **into Syriac**,
so that non-Greek-knowing Syrians could study the thinking.

It may be that al-Kindī & the Baghdadi translators
knew Syriac
& could look at some of Aristotle's *Metaphysics* in Syriac,
side by side with Plotinus' workings
from the same segments
of Aristotle's work in Greek.

If they didn't, it was more likely
a word that sat in the formal Greek language,
meaning one thing (to the Greek-speaking
philosophers?)
might've jumped
with a different meaning
into script & sound in Arabic
Peter Henry thinks.

Though not close, Syria was nearer to Baghdad
than Baghdad was to Greece. There were no aeroplanes
for a linguist, philosopher, or scholar to fly
between Athens & Baghdad at the time of al-Kindī.
Even now, Peter's met no Greek speakers on the streets
though he's encountered several Arabic-speaking Syrians
who also spoke English.
It was just before the mid-twentieth century in England
that Russell shared
what he knew of al-Kindī with Peter:
here, in Baghdad, Russell's knowledge leaves Peter full
of questions.

Though Peter hasn't read
the complicated arguments used to expound,
clarify,
          or differentiate
                    divergent, religious &/or theurgic positions
held by Pythagoreans, Platonists, Aristotelians, or Neo-Platonists,
he's noticed,   on at least some
early-twenty-first-century bookshelves,
many works in Arabic, which he's found out were *written by*
the early Arabic philosophers; then there are books *about them*,
in languages other than English
as well as books about them in English-as-a-first-language;
     & that there are
translations – from their works – into English, none of which
had been printed, hence weren't available
to Russell in the last century's late nineteen forties,
which was the only time Russell spoke to him about al-Kindī.

There was something Russell told him, then,
about al-Kindī, that Peter's scraps of current reading make him
     doubt.
The later studies that he's read assert al-Kindī *worked with...*
     or was part of...
a group or 'circle' of scholar-translators:
he philosophised but was not a translator.
Some of the translations they did were very free;
others went word by word, which Peter finds rather like
trying to catch the idea of a butterfly by its pieces,

instead of trying to sense what it did as a whole, looking
at how it moved,
watching how it flew.

There were no corresponding words in Arabic
for the Greek philosophical terms.
Al-Kindī had to find equivalents in his own language,
so others like himself
in the Arabic-speaking reading world
could share & work with new ideas, assimilate the new
knowledge.
Peter Henry Lepus suspects...that for him
to read Ya´qūb ibn Ishāq al-Kindī's writing in translation
might prove...too hard...But he wants to try. What
was it about?

Some facts Peter knows the words for, but does not necessarily 'translate' into 'meaning-full-ness', or understanding:

Al-Kindī died in the ninth century of the 'Christian Era', & was an Arab & a Muslim, who lived & taught in Baghdad under the ´Abbāsīd caliphate, which ruled Iran as well as Iraq, under the name of 'Persia'. He philosophised but was **not** a translator.

Aristotle, who was Plato's student, was born before the 'Christian Era' & so was not a 'Christian'. He & Plato spoke Greek together, which had words like '*philosophia*' in it, which al-Kindī & his circle had to 'think' into Arabic. '*Philosophia*' (the love of wisdom) eventually became '*falsafa*'.

Clifta has acquired a huge chart
with thirty-five characters on it
which she is busily running over
as if she is trying to learn Urdu script
by feeling for it
through her longer & now-always-cargo-pant-less legs.
It doesn't seem to be working.

The Urdu script's apparently the closest
she's been able to get, to Persian.
                                        Peter's read
that Persian script
is a modified form of Arabic,
(Persian, to him confusingly, is also called 'Farsi')
but that Urdu
            has sounds
            that don't occur
in Arabic or in Persian.

He's been to see an English-speaking 'language' expert,
philologist, & historian, in Abu Nuwas Street,
above a tiny room filled with cameras, to find out what,
if anything, is known
about the name 'Jamshýd', & emerged,
ears drooping, to gaze at the Tigris.

          (He's learnt no more about al-Kindī
          or the Egyptian-born,

Alexandria-dwelling philosopher
Plotinus, who 'founded Neo-Platonism',
travelled to 'Persia', fled,
& eventually
found 'sanctuary' in Rome
'protected' by Emperor Gallienus.

He'd been pondering
over the words of the poem
Clifta recited in the desert. It sank
into him, almost without his
noticing, owing to the many
& boring recitations
she gave.
He finds he
can remember it but does not
know what it looks like –
He has never seen it on a page.

He now has, spelt on a piece of paper,
the names 'Bahrám' & 'Jamshýd',
so he can spell them out or read them
in an anglicised script.

The *Rubáiyát*'s great Huntsman
has come out of the Persian language,
of a man called Omar Khayyám
who in turn

was 'translated'
into English
by a (part-Irish) Englishman
called Edward FitzGerald;

Clifta's mother's tales
of 'Arachnid Fitzgerald's translations'
puzzle Peter Henry Lepus mightily: *Did they come...previously...*
from the eleventh-century 'Persian' of Omar Khayyám,
or from the (Peter's found out*) very loose, English 'translations'*
of Edward FitzGerald – ;
Were they – are they still? – in 'spider'...a parallel text?...

A Suspension?

Clifta is not pleased with Peter.
She has begun to doubt
if he will EVER   help her
to leave Iraq. He notices
she spends more & more time
racing after tiny ants.
At first he thought
she was playing games with them
but she sprang at him so crossly
when he tried to come closer
to question her

that he decided not.

A Big Gold Map

Clifta has not told Peter
        WHERE
        in 'Persia'
she wants to go.

This, it turns out, has been
                a mistake, since it has led *him*
                to concentrate
                on how she might cross over
                onto 'Persian ground'
                & not to think at all
                of how much
                of it there is
                for her to travel on,
                nor how far in the wrong direction
                she might have to go
                if she needs to explore its far north.
                but enters from the lower 'Fertile Crescent',
                across from where
                the Hawr al-Hammar used to be,
                or from the Gulf end of the Shatt al-Arab,
which is even further south.

                There was a BIG gold map
                of the STATE OF IRAN
                which had blown away from the backpack.

Hamid had turned the camels,
dismounted, & collected it, &, Peter suspects,
though he's since seen Clifta crawling laboriously
over it, inspecting the back as well as the front,
she may not have noticed
she has approximately one thousand
two hundred & forty-eight kilometres
of shared border
from which to pick
her crossover point.

The problem, Peter has worked out,
from her silences, brief utterances,
& general crossness, is that
she herself does not know
where to begin her search.

Clifta's Spin

Clifta tells Peter
her mother carried them
around...   to guard

behind a rock...
in a sac of silk
she'd spun,

          & that
though Huntsman Spiders
like to run

across the barks of trees
& over city-humans' walls

they do   **not**   **not**
build aerial traps

nor send out   lines of silk
as if   to cross the world.

A Huntsman does not wait – in indolence –
by a web   as OTHER SPIDERS do
for leaf-aimed moths,
light flies,
or a clicking beetle
to blunder in.

He asks, *But what do Huntsman Spiders do?*
Clifta's legs stop their crab-like sideways jumps.
He thinks she's puzzled,
though he is not sure.
Her two
main eyes
        focus
                on him.
She says:
we stalk & ambush,
hide,   spring out   & pin our prey. We run.
We hunt the ground.

The Flowerbed Rabbit
once told Peter
how she's seen
Lady Spiders, low on webs
on dried but dew-wet grass,
entrap,
attack,
& eat
(while she was very close)
their anxious partners – leg by leg.

He remembers the Flowerbed Rabbit's
soft nose trembling, as she spoke,

& watching Clifta now, wondering

when she grows big & finds a mate   if she too
will eat...her kind, he asks:
Do Huntsman Spiders ever
eat...each other?

Clifta Tells...

        It turns out
she does not really know
what a Sydney Huntsman Spider
ought   to eat,   & perhaps
it is not   OTHER Spiders...
or   each other...

When Clifta & her siblings
first met light
they explored the differing textures
of their close-by earth, the white-splotched
bark & cockatoo-cut leaves
dropped
from the tree above,
& a grey-white
speckled granite rock, that was hard
to climb
for the tiny hatchlings' feet;
they did not watch their mother,
but felt the moves & flow of air
& listened to her as they crawled
& learnt to run.

Clifta says she never, then, saw
her mother hunt, but there was talk
of 'pinhead crickets' & much more...

In Australia, the little spider learned,
there are thirteen genera
& ninety-four species of Huntsman Spider.
Some – on trees –
hunt 'the gumleaf katydid' – or so
our mother said, but what that is
I do not know. We did not see her eat
when we were wrapped in silk & very small.
She hid us in our silken sac behind a rock   & guarded us
until we'd hatched, & for many weeks in which we grew.
I left, to seek, perhaps to find Bahrám,
before I found out all
of what I need to know...of what she knew...
She said our legs were made to move,
& that is what I do.

Braid

Max remembers the first time they made love
when she arrived travel-dusty & sweaty
after complications
getting from Basrah to Baghdad. Much afterwards
while they were lying together very close
she'd told him of a pet she'd had, when small:
had given it its scientific name – *Macropanesthia rhinoceros.*

It lived with them at Lismore, when Braid was a baby.
What else   was it known as?
                              Light-headed with relief –
Braid here beside him – Max hadn't felt the urge to ask:
    what was it?
nor to explain he didn't understand...classification's jargon...

Why,
    he'd asked instead,
                              was *she* called Braid?

Her face became unaccountably solemn.
Her mother'd had a long weekend
at Braidwood – way back in the late nineteen seventies –
it was after her uni exams'd finished – the finals –
she'd majored in chemistry – & she'd gone there for a
    long weekend
with her boyfriend

just before she married Braid's dad.
She'd liked the name, & the place, she'd said;
the boyfriend she loved had left her & she met Braid's dad
who was older. To think about whether she wanted to
    marry him,
she'd gone for a trip up north first, travelling alone to visit
    her family;
she'd acquired the *Macropanesthia rhinoceros* on the way back.
It had lived...Braid uttered thoughtfully...till she was
    almost seven.
A giant female rhinoceros cockroach. It took
two & a half Arnott's Milk Arrowroot biscuits

to balance evenly, matching weight with it   on the old
    apothecary's metal scales
(once used, her mother said, with the tiny metal weights on
    one side,
to weigh some long-ago-chemist's powders on the other) now
    in use
on the kitchen table.
Macropanesthia rhinoceros (Order: Blattodea) lived just outside
    their kitchen door
in the subterranean tunnels it made
in a large wooden box, nearly as tall as five-year-old Braid,
& only came up to the surface earth to bustle about when
    it rained.
Her dad made a fine-wire-mesh lid for the box,
to keep its inmate from predators

or escape. It took the rained-on leaf mulch
from the surface down below, making trip after trip
to feed its children.
Putting his leg across hers to stop the *récit*
as he enters her Max wonders
why is she telling me this?

Getting to Know

Why did you stop
working for the ABC? Braid asks.
There were people doing it better, Max says simply.
They didn't want me anymore.
I was doing radio interviews from Baghdad
during the advance, after
'Shock & Awe' – before the US tanks rolled in
& Baghdad's 'Fall'. It was hard for anyone
to get a line in. Now, I've had it with the War.
Naked
lying on the big double bed, one arm
twined round him, Braid is curious.
How've you been earning a living since?
Are you doing a story on Josh? Max strokes
the side of his neck reflectively conscious it feels
unusually smooth, except for the love bite. He's been to a
    barber, had his first
shave since the last
trip to the desert,
begged the use of a Spanish reporter's hotel room
borrowed some oddly-ill-fitting clean clothes
& managed to fluke, at the time it was hot, a shower,
all before Braid arrived. They've been in bed for nearly
    twelve hours.
Thinking he loves her, he answers rather uncomfortably.
    Turns out

he's been writing
'soft & squishy' travel pieces, 'scenic bullshit'
about 'small, safely-out-of-the-way places'
he's visited – years before – so all the information's
on the stale side – some of it likely rancid –
as promos for a well-heeled travel agency that sells package trips

to bottom, top, & middle ends of the market
& is 'strategically situated' with offices
at Chatswood, Burwood, & Botany.

She tells him Weasel has a long-held scheme –
if Max sends him a 'hot'
news or feature story from Iraq,
he'll *market it* under his 'Botany Jones' by-line,
& tell Max *nobody wanted it*.
Slightly ashamed, Braid adds,
she...hasn't mentioned this before
because Max...hasn't sent Weasel...
anything likely...
Her face, Max reads, is asking:
how will he take this? He shrugs. *Things've changed*, he says.
He didn't really *ever trust Weasel*.
He's not going to do a story on Josh
or on the nineteenth-century (Max's concluded 'lunatic'
– whether visionary
or schizophrenic) Mormon. He feels, he says, Josh's story is
too sad

& that Josh   whom he now counts as a friend
is 'crumbling' – as a person –   Besides,
he wants to tackle the 'better-brained' eco-tourism market,
might do some good for the countries & wildlife
a well-researched piece serves. He's done one already, that
found a market.
Sleepily, Braid wonders if he wants to work with her.

This Poem...

He guesses it was written
by an Australian serving in Iraq,
& **alive** after Baghdad's Fall,
this poem:

Bird-old,
cloud-young,
colour of scarlet,

trunk cicatrised
like the others around it:

blossoming gum.

The poem has no signature.
It's done in black.
Smaller, & far away
from the poem's end, in crayon-red
the name R Jackson has been scrawled,
(then, Raymond Terrace, Australia)
in letters Peter sees
were made by a different hand.

He's found this poem on a wall
beside a grey, still-lavender-bell-less jacaranda
by the Tigris, near where Republican Guards
– under heavy fire –

tore their uniforms off & throwing themselves on chance
& more deeply, on Allah's balancing mercy,
jumped into that black, flame-lit river
to escape the Allied Attack, though,
as Max had remarked, much later, to Braid,
foreign reporters (themselves at risk, that night,
from both sides' fusillades of fire & missiles
as were all Baghdadis)
observed that few Republican Guards could swim;
many were later washed up drowned.
Fresh water's not buoyant like salt.
You'd need to know how to float, hit no currents or snags,
to survive without swimming, Max'd said,
disguising his queasy empathy.
Putting one hand on the back of his neck
he'd disclosed an experience.
Dropped in a dam, aged six, to try to learn how to
float, he'd sunk,
opened his mouth to cry out but breathed-in water
& been choke-close to permanent failure
when his father dived down to mud & hauled him out.

Looking into the Tigris now
Peter thinks about snags & drowning.
He's seen shags perch – as if on nothing –
where underwater branches snarled the Murray
& he's heard the men, who live in shanties on its banks,
discuss old bits of jagged pipe

& cast-out beds with metal spikes
that cut their fishing lines & when the water levels fell
impaled a diver.

Remembering Max's words Peter shivers.

He thinks back to the poem on the wall.
He doubts he knows what '**bird-old**' means.

'**cloud-young**'...
A young cloud...must be new.
Young clouds have not come yet.
The sky above the wall is cloudless blue.

He's had to look up '**cicatrise**',
traverse Baghdad,
get back to his dictionary
to understand that part of the poem.
Returned to the wall
by the Tigris
he thinks of scars –

that no foot, claw or paw
can leave on water.

'**blossoming gum**'

These words make Peter think of the Flowerbed Rabbit

her gazing up, crouched at the base
of it – '**colour of scarlet**' –
the one they saw once, travelling together,
all the gums scarred
but only one flowering. They'd needed
to leave it,
going nowhere in particular,
her showing him the coastal grasses, away from
roads & rifles,
heading out.

Braid's Book

Braid brought in
to Baghdad with her,
Sydney-purchased,
a lonely planet travel guide
to Iran, which she
left behind
in Josh's
second wife's bedroom
where she'd slept with Max.
Max rescued it. Peter found it
on the back floor
of the car Josh hired
to drive her, him & Max
to Babylon. They've been already
several times, Max & Josh to search for Josh's absent
    Mormon wives
as well as for the plates inscribed with Mormon law
while Braid went salt-marsh-desertwards alone.
Peter remembers
she said she didn't
need her book yet, *not*
for this trip to the Delta,
though *It might be useful*
later, if I need to cross
the Shatt al-Arab. A boat's
in Iranian water

once it's more than
halfway across the Shatt. If that happens,
I've got an Iranian visa, so it should be o.k.
I thought I might
go to Iran proper, next trip, to see what I can find out
about the vegetation
& wildlife's state,
(& status),
on the waterway's other side.

Josh barely listened. Lost
in his own dark ponderings, about his loves...Could the two youngest
have passed as Iranian Muslims, immersed within the stream of those
devout & penitent returnees   flowing back across the border to Iran,
returning from pilgrimage to the holy
city of Karbala – & thus...alive...have been allowed
to leave Iraq   without visa? Would   it be practical to entertain this hope?

Does he   deserve   to find them?
Only Peter heard him muttering about this. Max
was gazing at Braid absorbed in her plans.

The book is made with EXTRA STRENGTH
so it will not crack – easily – in a backpack

Designed for a human's hand,
too heavy for Peter to grip, though he can page-turn
with ease, it is small & chunky
with a shining bird's-eye-black-
&-gloss-gold cover,
a gold that reminds him also – unexpectedly – of corn
the unchewed knobs of which – in rain –
have such a shine.
Disappointingly,
there are not many pictures of grass in the book,
& – in the photographs there are – the grass is
brown
like some he glimpsed
near Cooma once,
when he was too far above, standing on his hind legs
on the window seat of a near-empty plane
flying at ten thousand metres,
to tell what kind of grass it was.
                                        Braid'd remarked
on the grass in the pictures, too, to Max but including Josh:
                                        nothing like
the high-rainfall grasses of coastal Queensland
where her mother came from,
                                   nor
the verdant tussocks round the banana plantation out
   from Lismore,
                                   where *she*
grew up.

Josh, turned inward, seemed scarcely to register
Braid's voice

but he might have taken in,
subliminally,

the photos' desert-like grass.
He'd muttered,
There was a man in the eighteen-eighties in Salt Lake City
talked of
in a soldier's history,
recorded as having twenty wives
with twenty bedrooms, one for each;
then, in the City of Mormons if a man
with twenty wives gave a tythe
of ten per cent of what he made or grew
to the Church & only slept with a wife
to make a child,
*& did not sleep with a wife '**with child**', nor with her*
for nine months after the babe was born, that man...
was not 'in sin',
he was considered 'a good Mormon'.
He'd quietly groaned, *The Utah doctor said*
that I had lazy sperm...in ten years...with fifteen wives...
no pregnancies now, one...
& she who
when she left
was carrying my child
may already be...with God.

'Zarathustra'?...
Only a Draft

As to 'gods', I have no means of knowing either that they exist or that they do not exist. For many are the obstacles that impede knowledge, both the obscurity of the question and the shortness of the questioner's life. PROTAGORAS

A young arts student in Australia
who has 'translated' some
of Protagoras' writings – he claims, 'very badly' –
specially, for Peter Henry,
has sent, with them, the addenda: 'Protagoras,
a citizen of Abdere, was born, perhaps,
in four nine 0
or four eight one B.C.
& is biographed, by two esteemed historians,
as having lived (probably) until (almost) seventy...'

Peter Henry Lepus has copied this,
plus the 'translation' from Protagoras,
with a felt-tipped pen, carefully
into his wind-torn desert notebook.

He has slowly come to the conclusion
that all the Pre-Socratics
seem to have been human;
he can find no reference
to support his notion

that any of them
were rabbits. He will have to redraft
some of his 'lives', he thinks,
but, elsewhere at least, there may be 'rabbits'
to read it.
He does not doubt 'The World'
is full of 'rabbits' wanting to read...

Before his arrival in 'two 0 0 three Iraq',
he'd pawed, & pored over,
a few of the lower shelf's reachable newer books
in the small Philosophy section
of a Sydney public library, to try
to find out how to write an introduction
short in duration
as a small, fresh, un-rabbit-chewed
square of green grass. Having read some
succinct, though widely-branched, delicate
introductory summations of those books' directions,
he's been forced by his thoughts,
during the long journey to the watered Euphrates,
to reject the idea
that the opening chapter...(on where things are hopping to
in the lives of philosophers, whose writings
span more than two millennia...)
should be constructed as one paragraph,
perhaps no larger than a Shetland pony's hoof print.

Having left Clifta, temporarily ensconced
in the relative – at any rate,
when he left her, roofed – security of Josh Smith's kitchen
in Baghdad,
Peter's begun to draft, with a sense of uneasy relief,
the Introduction
to his
History of Philosophers
                    for Rabbits;
he's adapted, with some misgivings,
the ideas
of the early (pre-Christian) philosopher, Protagoras,
who was, Peter feels, somewhat
ignorant
of the existential needs of THE RABBIT,
since his text
is addressed
unequivocally,
to MAN.
        Peter Henry hopes
not to make, through his own
        unconscious assumptions,
a similar mistake.

        His position is, he feels,
                both more precarious
                        & more dubious

than that of the early
philosophising Greek.
Who wrote:
Man...
is the measure of all things, of things
that are as they are, & of things that are not
that they are not:
which, Peter guesses,
was not written, originally, in English
& perhaps... will need to be
'translated'
into Australian English for Australian rabbits
if his proposed book for Cambridge University Press
is to reach readers there.
There has been some talk about 'niche marketing'
which he does not fully understand.
He ponders on a sat-phone-call he had in Baghdad
from his distant relation, Picasso Rabbit, who, in between
chewing mouthfuls of wet Lake District grass, kindly relayed
an email from a worried Cambridge
scholar: *With regard*
to your proposed
'History of Philosophers':

Will
the
language
you

propose
to use

be comprehended

by the Australian rabbit?

Gazing thoughtfully out
from a dark rock outcrop west of Babylon,
across the paler camel-colours of the desert
which extends as far west as he can see,
between patches of short, shrubby ground-hugging plants –
that he has found, in the normally dry, Iraqi desert-summer,
not at all tasteful to eat, he writes:
Education
        does not grow
like the first plantings of Brussels sprouts
in the winter-chilled grounds
of the rural
British rabbit
until
        much time
                has passed.

The acquisition of knowledge
needs natural gifts, & practice;
a rabbit must begin

to learn

in his or her

early youth.

Philosophical ideas

do not sprout

in the rural rabbit's consciousness –

nor, indeed, in any mind –

until education has taken root

(those roots gone down)

& something called

'great depth'

is reached.

He is alone, in a place of no sound.
He pauses, nose wrinkled, sniffing
the dry western desert air, that, for all he knows,
may be smelt...as far away as silent Syria.
It is a long time
since the last century, when the sound
of Harry St John Philby's motorbike,
would have travelled through   or so Peter imagines.
Each silence is different. Then,
that British scholar, diplomat, map-maker & writer
was drawing lines, to make maps
that were to form, officially,
the 'boundaries'
of 'countries'. Russell
had told Peter, then, that the 'boundaries'

of 'countries'   may shift   as result   of 'war'.

He can see   no 'boundaries' on the sand
from where he squats,
as percipient, locked in, to the 'now'
of Gregorian calendar time –
late July, two thousand & three –
slightly south of Babylon. Furthermore, he does not like
the writing of
his Introduction's early draft.

He has travelled, during the night,
a considerable distance from the
enormous gold & green
pillared gates,
first built perhaps in the seventh century B.C.,
honouring '*Ishtar*',
who, so Peter's heard, on 'American Public Radio',
was *a fabled, Fertile Crescent*
Goddess of Love & War, whose 'Gates', from the days
of the mighty Babylonian warrior-king Nebuchadnezzar,
were rebuilt, late twentieth century,
by the then-current leader of Iraq.

Peter has left Josh & Max searching Babylon & surrounds
for traces of the golden plates – or any
of Josh's fourteen wives.
It seems one may have died

when a wall fell on her in a missile strike,
near the Tigris. Josh was too upset, not knowing
which of his fifteen wives
it was, only that...it was thought 'likely'
it was one of them. After his initial
requests made in shock brought no answers
he'd become unable to talk on the phone,
or to repeat any of his questions without crying.

Max who's tried to check persistently
since *he* took over the enquiries
has failed for weeks
to get I.D. confirmed,
or to locate the body.
What he's eventually told,
he does not tell Josh all of –
no teeth, face, hair,
skin – or fingers –
& the legs were missing. No one, it seemed,
'd had the interest – or time – to do a post-mortem.
Cause of death was known, no DNA swab taken.
It had not been recorded   if the body was pregnant...
They cannot permit
'the American brother'   to come to view... it is – 'too late'...

Joshua, meanwhile,
has managed to convince himself
some of his wives too

are looking for the plates,
& travelling south.

Max has come to believe –
if the plates exist – they're likely the work
of an early twentieth-century
Milwaukee master-forger.
Braid has left them
to travel back to Ur, & beyond – to investigate the salt marshes
& collect more information about the effects of deaths
of brine-tolerant plants on the Delta's declining fauna.
Max,
when Peter last saw him, was grumpy.
He doesn't like Braid out of his sight, even though she's
travelling
in traditional Iraqi-female dress. He's worried some good-looking
fast-talking lecherous Spanish, Polish, Indian, or British
photographer
might 'latch on to her'...She's got 'a University degree', &
'likes 'em smart'.
'Ambitious, too. Dead-keen
on getting her environment piece done right.'

Peter's heard him confessing his worries to
an older Australian Pan-Arabist journalist friend; 'she's brighter
than I am. I only feel
okay when we're alone in bed'.

Weasel
has knocked back his idea for a feature story
on an extinct species of Delta fish.
'You can't get people worked up
about something that isn't there anymore. No editor
would touch it.'

End Notes

On December 13th 2003 Saddam will be captured and handed over for trial by Iraqis.

On December 26th 2003 Iran will suffer the horrendous Bam earthquake. Approximately 43,000 people will die, as a result of it and there will be approximately 20,000 wounded and 60,000 left homeless.

Where the dramatis personae of this book will be then is unknown.

The world is all that is the case (referred to in 'Journeys West of "War"', p. 145). This is the translation of Proposition 1 of Wittgenstein's *Tractatus Logico-Philosophicus* by D.F. Pears and B.F. McGuinness from the 1974 Routledge & Kegan Paul paperback edition, which includes Bertrand Russell's 'Introduction' to the first English translation made by C.K. Ogden with the assistance of F.P. Ramsey in 1922.

Although he has sat in on numerous deep discussions of the *Tractatus*, its small numbered segments involving many hours of talk, Peter has only encountered the 1974 paperback edition of the Pears-McGuinness translation.

Ludwig Wittgenstein was born in 1889 and died in 1951. Bertrand Russell was born in 1872 and died in 1970.

Names:

Al Shualla – an imaginary location that may or may not relate to an actual one which is spelled differently.
sat-phone – satellite phone
sat-dish – satellite dish

Satellite phones and satellite dishes were used in Iraq in 2003 for out-of-the-country phone calls by those journalists and others lucky enough to be able to access them. (Mobile phones with aerials were sold in Baghdad shortly after the Coalition forces occupied it.)

Iran used to be called 'Persia'. Like Farsi, the name 'Persia' is derived from Fars Province in Iran, where Aryan tribes settled. The use of the name 'Iran' is relatively modern and was introduced under Reza Shah in 1934/35. Meaning 'of noble origin', 'Iran' has its roots in the word Aryan.

'Persia': the name used in books about ancient civilizations, their arts, cultures or significant philosophers: the land area it refers to is much broader than that occupied by contemporary Iran (which itself has been described as 'more than twice as big as Texas', *Iran and Iraq Nations at War,* Lisa Mannetti, Franklin Watts, 1986).

As Peter Henry has discovered in his readings, the boundaries of 'Persia' have fluctuated over 'Time': the 'Persian Empire', which was established under the Achaemenids, stretched from north-west India to the eastern Mediterranean. It was created, according to the *Cambridge Paperback Encyclopaedia* (ed. David Crystal), in the second half of the sixth century B.C. and overthrown in 330 B.C. by Alexander the Great (of Macedon).

As Peter Henry eventually found out, through more reading, the early 'Greek' philosophers who travelled to 'Persia' in the period may have gone no further east than Babylon, or 'Babylonia', in Iraq.